LOST, BUT FOUND

Also by Cheryl Wilfong

- 2013 *Every Good Thing*
- 2012 *Impermanent Immortality*
- 2011 *At the Mercy of the Elements*
- 2010 *That Rascal Mind*
- 2010 *The Meditative Gardener: Cultivating Mindfulness of Body, Feelings, and Mind*
- 2008 *Passacaglia on Passing*
- 2007 *Off the Beaten Track*
- 2006 *Scattered Clouds*
- 2006 *Following the Nez Perce Trail: A Historical Guide to the Nee-Me-Poo National Historic Trail with Eyewitness Accounts (2nd ed.)*
- 2005 *Roasted Chestnuts*
- 2003 *Hot Flashes*
- 2002 *Light Fingers*
- 1999 *India Journal*

LOST, BUT FOUND

CHERYL WILFONG

2014

Cheryl Wilfong
Heart Path Press, L3C
314 Partridge Road
Putney VT 05346

www.meditativegardener.com

©2014 Cheryl Wilfong
All rights reserved. No part of this book may be
reproduced in any form or by any means, electronic
or mechanical, including photocopying, recording,
or by any information storage and retrieval system,
without permission in writing from the publisher.

ISBN: 978-0-9825664-6-6

Follow The Meditative Gardener *on Facebook*

My Dear Friend,

Welcome to the 2014 edition of my writings.

The upside of losing things is having enough space in your life to find something else. I don't know about you, but for myself, I've always had to close the door on the past good and tight before a new door opens, revealing a possibility I had never imagined. Lose the old, so that there's enough breathing space for the new to make its appearance, to be "found".

As usual, the Warning Label reads:

— WARNING —

You may think you know the characters in these writings, but if you ask the people with those names, you'll hear a completely different story.

I really loved working with my sister, Dona Fuller, on several of the memoir pieces. Thanks to Mike Fleming, the editor of this volume, who kindly pushes me to write more deeply and more thoroughly and to finally write the endings to many of these stories. I remain grateful to Jan Frazier and her writing groups in which the first drafts of most of these pieces were written. Jenny Holan, proofreader extraordinaire, scrubs my manuscript clean. Oh! Does that feel good. As always, deep affection and appreciation go to this book's designer, Carolyn Kasper.

> Cheryl Wilfong
> cheryl.wilfong@gmail.com

CONTENTS

BILL & CHERYL

Lost and Found	3
Finding	19
A Good Deed a Day	21
Togetherness	23
Silent Sonata	25
Falling in Love with Mabel	26

TRAVEL

San Juan Island	31
Micah in Mexico	35
August Vacation	37
My Tent	40
Pack River Store	43

CHERYL'S MEMORIES

Racing	49
Playing College	52
The Difference between Men and Women	55
Treasurer	59
Bookkeeping	61
Cheryl (Also)	64
Social Anxiety	66
Jungian Analysis	68
Family Meetings	71

LIFE

The Plan	83
Louisa von Trapp	86
What Is Family, Anyway?	88
The Oedipal Complex	91
Community Thanksgiving	94
Pine Ridge	96
East Hillside	100
Heat Pump	102
Milk of Human Kindness	105
Facebook Photos of Our Nearest and Dearest	109

Not Facebooking	111
Valuation	114
Four Classes at the Circus School	118
Stretching	122
Thinning Hair	125
Wreckage	128
Tibetan Prayer Wheel	130
Lou's Memorial Service	133

BEST OF THE BLOG 2014
The Heavenly Messengers
137

DHARMA TALKS

It's All in the Company You Keep	161
The Complete Streets of Our Spiritual Path	163
Forgive Them	165
In Conclusion	167

BILL & CHERYL

LOST AND FOUND

CHAPTER 1

Sunday, September 8

WE LEFT THE WEDDING reception on Camano Island at 4:10. The invitation had said 1:00–5:00, but by four, the festivities were winding down. The 59-year-old bride, Joyce, and the 62-year-old groom, Roger—his first marriage—had reported on their weeklong cruise in the San Juan Islands on a 42-foot sailboat. Rick, the captain and our host for the reception, had married Joyce and Roger on Orcas Island a couple of days earlier, when the sun had shone for an hour.

That was the day Bill and I had been biking on Lopez Island, so we knew what the weather had been—a lot of thunderstorms, complete with distant lightning. After a couple of hours on bicycles that rainy morning, we had stopped at the only supermarket on the island to dry out.

Captain Rick's wife, Anita—the cruise director and Joyce's best friend from grade school—had forgotten to bring the marriage certificate on board, so the couple signed the document in the garden, followed by the two witnesses, Chef Frances and her significant other, Jerry, whom Joyce had introduced to each other ten years earlier. Then Captain Rick invited the rest of us to sign the certificate as well, our signatures floating off the bottom of the document.

The catered food from a Whole Earth market was delicious, the carrot cake a bit too sweet. Toasts had been made by the groom's brother and sisters and the bride's best friends, who had been with her through thick and thin.

We had started playing croquet but were distracted by conversation. Then there was nothing left to do but schmooze, so I raised my eyebrows to Bill, and he nodded. It was a good time to depart.

First we had to drive off Camano Island via the bridge over the spectacular Deception Pass and onto Fiderio Island. By 4:30 on Sunday afternoon, hundreds of Seattleites were winding up their September weekend and avoiding the ferry and its two-hour wait at the south end of Camano Island, so traffic was heavy as we bridged onto the mainland and through Arlington, Washington.

At 5:10, we stopped to fill up with gas, and that's when Bill discovered his wallet was missing.

Had he dropped it in the grassy field where we parked our car? He called Anita and Rick. They would go look.

Since Bill loses either his wallet, keys, credit card, cell phone, hat, or jacket at least once a month, I know the drill. I pulled into an empty bank parking lot and took everything out of the rental car.

By this time in our travels, the back seat was a regular storage unit: sneakers and hiking boots on the floor along with a bag of travel snacks and some cans of seltzer. The back seat itself was covered with jackets, day packs, travel literature, and, on Bill's side, the passenger side, a selection of hats.

Everything out, and then everything closely examined before it went back into the car. I actually wanted to look at every single thing myself, but after making his phone call, Bill did his side while I did mine.

Oh, I wanted to continue driving eastward so badly. We were headed across the North Cascades Highway, a spectacular road through the mountains that I hadn't traveled since 36 years earlier. It would be a winding, slow road to get to my sister's home in the Idaho panhandle, but oh-so-green and mountainous.

But how would we get on the airplane on Thursday if Bill didn't have his wallet and, by extension, his driver's license?

This is the way Bill eventually finds everything he has lost. He retraces his steps over the past few days, calls every store he has been in, revisits the Latchis Theater mid-morning, or Brown and Roberts hardware store. I knew that my journey across the North Cascades was doomed. I had thought that if we had a two-hour head start, we could get as far as Concrete, Washington, before dark. Then we'd have only eight hours to drive the next day. Now, we would lose our head start and have to go via Interstate 80, a mere six-hour drive.

"Bill, do you not want to go to Idaho to see my sister?" I asked. Bill, you see, is a somatic guy. His body acts out feelings he is too ashamed to admit. It used to be that I'd come home from a week away to find him flat on his back. He had felt abandoned, but didn't want to tell me. So instead, his back went out.

He also has a difficult time making transitions. Maybe he wasn't ready to leave the wedding even though he seemed to be? Maybe he really wanted to party on?

We drove back to Camano Island. As we approached Anita and Rick's house, I said, "Bill, look at the road carefully. Sometimes you put things on top of the car. Maybe it blew off." I drove slowly down the road and into the driveway, our eyes scanning the road and the weeds alongside.

I reparked the car where we had been two hours earlier. Bill searched; I searched. No luck. We went indoors, where the Captain and Anita were still entertaining Frances and Jerry and another friend, Sharon. I went to the bathroom. I confirmed with Captain Rick that, now that we would be headed south, the best escape route was still an hour's drive northward.

"Oh, yes," he said. "That North Cascades Highway is closed anyway, due to four or five landslides." Well, we couldn't have driven the North Cascades Highway anyway. Maybe Bill's lost wallet saved us from that?

We drove back across Deception Pass, across Fiderio Island to the mainland.

"I need to go to the bathroom," Bill said as the sun set. I pulled into a Walgreens, and while Bill was in the store I went through his side of the back seat again, including his day pack—the front section, the middle section, the main section.

And there it was: his wallet.

CHAPTER 2

Friday, September 13

WE FLEW FROM SPOKANE to Salt Lake City on Thursday. My plan was to drive southeast and head toward Canyon Country, but Bill couldn't take his eyes off the Wasatch mountains. The eastern boundary of Salt Lake City is the Wasatch fault, then—*boom!*—you're in the mountains.

Salt Lake looks like I had expected Denver to look. But mile-high Denver is on the plains, and the Rocky Mountains are thirty miles away in the blue-sky distance. In Salt Lake City, the mountains are right there, thirty blocks east of the Mormon temple downtown.

The Wasatch are powder mountains, filled with ski resorts like Alta and Sundance. The next day, we moseyed through the mountains and took a three-hour hike, beginning at 6,500 feet and winding up at 7,800 feet.

Back in our car, we rambled on past other ski resorts, over Guardsman Pass in the fog, surprisingly, because the fall of 2013 had seen a tremendous amount of rain in Utah and Colorado. When we had floated through the Grand Canyon ten years earlier, I heard about what northern Arizonans call the "monsoon season." I imagined a dark cloud on the horizon, from which fell slanted gray rain. Even though it might be thirty miles away, there would be enough rain to flash-flood some arroyo—maybe the one you just happened to be standing in. But my experience of that western monsoon season 2013 was more like a deluge, and it began with cloud cover so low that we had absolutely no view at all from Guardsman Pass.

A little way down the eastern flank, our narrow road forked. Heber City? Or Park City? The Utahns like to city-fy their small towns.

Bill, the driver of the hour, chose the wider Park City road, and we soon found ourselves in that skiing mecca. A small town, heavily boutiqued, with an outdoor store in every neatly designed shopping plaza. Not our kind of place. We headed out of town with me at the wheel, found U.S. 40, and started driving southeast when a deluge hit. I put the windshield wipers on full speed and still couldn't see much. Western drivers zoomed past me. "I'm getting off at the next exit," I said.

Bill nodded. It was four in the afternoon, time to look for a place to stay for the night.

The Inn at Stillwater beckoned. It turned out to be a time-share, not really a hotel. The bedroom was rather small, so I sat propped up in bed, paging through travel literature and feeling confined. "Hey, look Bill. Here's a brochure for a Friday Night Film Series. We could go to a movie tonight."

He was tired, but I was champing at the bit. Now that it was evening, the low sun was slanting across the wet landscape beautifully.

We drove back the nine miles to Park City, had dinner at the deli in the Green Supermarket, and then went off to find the film series at the library.

The 1930s building had "Park City High School" on the façade, but it had now been repurposed for municipal uses such as library, day-care center, and University of Utah extension.

We climbed up to the third floor and found a dozen volunteers staffing the film series: two ticket sellers, a popcorn seller (bring your own bowl and save a dollar), a cookie seller, a ticket taker.

We walked into the 516-seat-capacity theater. This is one of the auditoriums where the Sundance Film Festival takes place every January. That night there were only a few dozen people, but the mood was friendly and local. The movie ended before ten, and then we headed back to the Inn at Stillwater.

As I was thinking about bed, Bill said, "My wallet's missing. It must be at that movie theater. We have to drive back to Park City now."

"Bill, the library building closes at ten," I sighed.

"Maybe someone will be there cleaning up," he said.

"Why, oh why, didn't I take a photo of your driver's license while you had it?" I moaned.

We drove the fifteen minutes back to Park City. Bill banged on the doors of the library building. It was too dark outside and too dim inside the car for me to really examine the car for his wallet. I rested my forehead on the steering wheel. It was an hour past my bedtime. Was losing his wallet a way for Bill to be passive-aggressive? To silently say *I didn't want to go to that damn movie anyway, and now I'm going to get even with you?*

Finally Bill returned and said, "Let's come back in the morning."

"Okay," I said. "The library doesn't open until ten."

As we drove back to the Inn at Stillwater, Bill reviewed the possibilities. "These hiking pants have shallow pockets," he said. "I think the wallet dropped out of my seat at the movies."

We were in bed by 11:15, and next morning we arrived at the library building at 9:30. The outside door was open, and Bill went in but returned a few minutes later. "Bring a flashlight," he said. "The auditorium is dark."

We explored the auditorium with our flashlights. "The popcorn's been swept up," I said.

I went back to the car, while Bill went looking for the maintenance person. He knocked on the library door and a librarian said, "We're not open yet. Ten o'clock."

Bill motioned to her though the window in the door.

He came back to the car with three names and phone numbers and began to call them on my cell phone. He left messages with the property-management company and with the film series contact person. Then he called the police department. "Did someone turn in a wallet? My name is William McKim."

"Yes, someone turned it in last night. It's in an evidence locker, but we can't open it until Monday, when a detective comes in."

Well, did we want to come back on Monday and get it? Or drive on to Moab and pick it up on Thursday on our way to the airport at Salt Lake City? Are things in evidence lockers really safe? Or do they have a tendency to disappear?

I knew Bill would be anxious every single hour that

he didn't have his wallet in his possession. And I voted for a Monday morning pickup because if anything went haywire, we'd have a few days to call the Vermont Department of Motor Vehicles and try to get a copy of his driver's license FedExed to us before flying home on Friday.

"Okay, then," I said. "Let's drive east to Dinosaur National Monument and then go up to Flaming Gorge. That means we'll be back here tomorrow night. We can go to the police department Monday morning, and *then* we'll drive to Canyonlands."

Bill nodded.

"Okay then," I said. "Since we'll be driving through Roosevelt, Utah, I want to stop there and visit Dad's army buddy, Lynn."

I called up whitepages.com on my iPhone, typed "Lynn Labrum" into People Search, saw the phone number, and tapped it.

"Hello."

"Hi, Lynn. This is Cheryl Wilfong." I paused a moment for my name to register with him.

"Wilfong," he repeated. "That's a familiar name. Who did you say you are?"

"Cheryl. I'm Ralph's oldest daughter. I'm the one who was a VISTA volunteer in Cedar City, Utah in 1970."

"Oh, you're the one who went astray. Your dad thought you were on Poverty Row."

My eyes were suddenly damp to hear my dad spoken of so familiarly.

"I'm in Park City now, and I'd like to drop in and visit you this afternoon."

"Well, I'm living in assisted living. I call it a jail without bars."

"Could I drop in this afternoon?"

"Sure."

"How long will it take to drive to Roosevelt?" I asked.

"A couple of hours. Our football team just played Park City last night. Did you see it?"

"No, I sure didn't," I said. "So I'll see you in a couple of hours, then."

And I was suddenly glad, very glad, that Bill had lost his wallet.

CHAPTER 3

Saturday, September 21

WE'D BEEN HOME FROM the Lost-Wallet-x-2 Trip for less than 24 hours when Bill called me from Brown and Roberts hardware store.

Actually, he called me twice. The first time was to consult with me about buying a new chainsaw. He had taken his/our 23-year-old Stihl in for yet another tune-up.

Just that morning he'd been clearing the ski trails with the neighbors, and I could see that it was taking him much too long to saw through a ten-inch-diameter beech that had fallen across the brook and onto a little ski bridge. He'd just had the chainsaw in for repairs before we left on our trip.

"Paul here tells me I should consider a new saw," Bill said.

I do a quick mental calculation. Bill is 77. Let's see, 77 plus 23 is 100, and I sure hope he's not still using a chain saw at that age.

I keep expecting him to retire from chainsawing, but this is the guy who at eleven years old was president of his self-created Woodsman Club that included a couple of his buddies. As long as he is competent, it does seem like he should have the right tools.

"Okay," I say. "You can charge it to my account, and I'll give it to you for your 78th-birthday present." This is one of the beauties of a hometown hardware store. I still have the charge account I set up there in 1979, when I was building the house I live in and using the Homelite chainsaw my dad had bought for me.

Five minutes later, I received a second phone call from Bill. "I've lost my keys," he said.

"Lost your keys? At Brown and Roberts? How did that happen?"

"I must have put them down on the counter, and someone else picked them up, thinking they were their keys."

Bill loves to lay things down in a "convenient" place, like the nice flat roof of the car.

I have not, in 25 years, been able to understand how Bill's organizing efforts fail him. I believe in putting things in a predictable place so that I can find them again. For me, it's a matter of efficiency. Keys in my right pocket. Then I know where to find them after a moment—or many—of mindlessness.

But Bill, it seems, prefers the convenience method. He just can't always remember, five minutes or five hours later, where "convenient" was, even though he tries to practice mindfulness.

"Can you come get me?" he asked.

"Okay," I sighed.

I got into my Prius, and backed out of the garage before I remembered it would be a good idea to take Bill's second set of keys with me. Otherwise, I'd have to make two trips: one to pick him up and one to deliver him back to his car. Oh, yes, I prefer efficiency whenever possible.

I took his key to him in town. It was only forty minutes out of my day, I told myself. I was so close to finishing my manuscript for my annual book of reflections, but now, I could see, it wouldn't happen today.

The next morning, Sunday, Bill went to work, playing the organ at the Christian Science church. Afterward, he drove to Brown and Roberts, and there were his keys. They'd been turned in.

Wallet, wallet again, then keys. My metaphorical mind seeks the meaning in these weekly losses.

CHAPTER 4

Saturday, September 28

AND THEN, THE FOLLOWING Saturday evening, I met Bill at Actors Theater for their Ten-Minute Play Festival. I was coming from a workshop in Boston, and he was coming from the annual meeting of his favorite anti-nuclear group.

I arrived early and saved him a seat. When he arrived, he visited for a minute with our friends, Paul and Karen, sitting in front of us, and then said he was going downstairs for a cookie.

"Hey Bill, I've got two cookies in my car from the workshop I was at today," I said.

Bill McKim, being Scotch, always prefers the less expensive option.

"Here's the key to my car," I said.

He returned smiling. We watched three ten-minute plays. At intermission, he decided to go home He was so tired, and he had to play the organ at church in the morning. I stayed for the second set of the next three ten-minute plays.

Then, as I was bidding farewell to Paul and Karen, I put my hand in my right front pocket. My empty pocket. "I don't have my car key," I said.

"Cookies," said Karen. "Bill has your key."

The last ten-minute play, entitled "Philadelphia," was about a guy who can't find what he wants—the drugstore doesn't have aspirin, the news vendor doesn't have his favorite paper. His friend tells him he's in a Philadelphia. "You can never find what you want when you're in a Philadelphia." Meanwhile, his mellow friend in a Hawaiian shirt and flip-flops is in a "Los Angeles" and is utterly unruffled when he hears that he's been fired from his job and that his wife has left him.

I felt I must be suffering from a "Lost Vegas." I could call it a Whidbey or a Park City, or a Brattleboro. Or maybe I was just suffering from a "Bill-adelphia."

EPILOGUE

Ever the seeker for meaning, I really don't know which way to go, which conclusions to jump to with all these losts and eventually founds.

Do all Bill's losts simply teach me patience? Patience with life as it unfolds in the present moment? Patience because things are not going the way I want them to? Is that it?

More often I feel like I'm stuck in Bill's bad dream. The kind of anxiety dream where the plane is leaving, and I'm still packing, looking for and not finding whatever is supposed to go in my luggage. I'm never going to make it.

Fortunately for me, I'm just a bit player in Bill's bad dream (if that's what it is), which is happening in real time. He's the one who's wracking his brains, wondering where he lost his wallet, his keys, his glasses, his credit card, his music. He's the one who suffers the anxiety. He's the one who calls every store he's been in, every church, every person he's seen.

Sometimes I wonder why in my airplane-packing dreams I don't just say "Screw this junk" and simply go get on the damn airplane. Who needs stuff anyway?

Sometimes, I think his losts are simply an excuse to connect with people, call them up, chat, ask about whatever was lost, and above all, relate. Maybe he's just feeling lonely and wants to talk to someone?

Is losing your wallet about losing your IDs? Losing your identity? Is losing his cash a sign that a fool and his money are soon parted?

Is losing the keys to your vehicle a metaphor for losing the ability to keep the body going? Losing control?

Is losing your honey bear a sign of losing your honey?

Or are all the losses telling me to slow down? Is he saying, *Don't drive me so fast, Cheryl. Relax. Kick back?* Even if you are doing all the driving because Bill has lost not only his wallet but his driver's license, and now you are the chauffeur. Is this his way of handing authority over to me?

Or is he stuck in a continual game of hide-and-seek? Replaying some old trauma, perhaps one he doesn't even remember, over and over and over again? The resolution never comes.

Are the losses Bill's way of asserting his right to be himself? Find himself?

When Bill loses something, I don't get anxious. That is so useless. It's his loss, his anxiety; it's up to him to find it.

Any number of times I have seen women jump in to help the minute Bill reports his missing fill-in-the-blank. While I stand back and enjoy the game, enjoy the show, other women are asking him all sorts of helpful questions. *Where did you last see it? When did you last have it? Then what did you do? Are you sure it's not in your pocket? Your jacket? Your luggage?* They even help him look.

Is that what he wants? Help? Help because he can't do it himself? Because he doesn't want to do it alone? Because he wants company, companionship? Because he wants some mommy to help him? Is this the way he gets Mommy's attention? Does he bask in the attention of being helped?

I simply know that Bill *will* find it. Eventually. Weeks or months later. I don't even need to look.

He will find his glasses lying on the edge of the lawn a year later. He will find his concert music notebook on the cinder block beside the furnace three weeks after he lost it and after he combed his files to make duplicate copies for his upcoming organ concert.

He will find whatever he has lost. Or he won't. And life goes on.

Maybe Bill is teaching me something about losses. Everything I own and call mine will eventually be lost to me—house, furniture, clothes, pictures. And one day, due to stroke or dementia and certainly after death, Bill and I will be lost to each other.

Often these losses come at an inconvenient time, a time not under my control. Impermanence, instability hits me over the head. *Pay attention.* This is one of the truths of life, one of life's deep lessons. Practice now with these small losses. Learn patience, compassion, equanimity. Practice now with these little losses because the big losses are coming soon enough.

FINDING

Let me celebrate a day of finding. Bill found his reading glasses at the bottom of his sock drawer. He tried to construct a story so that this storage place made sense. I leave it to you, dear reader, to make up your own story, which has an equal probability of being true.

The main thing is: Bill found his reading glasses—the ones he uses to read music. Since he spends three hours a day at the piano or the organ, you can readily understand that his reading glasses are quite important.

He assures me that he keeps one pair of his prescription reading glasses on his grand piano in his music studio, one pair upstairs next to his computer, and a third pair in his organ shoes, which he carries in his music bag as he traipses from church to church. The local Christian Science church, where he plays most Wednesday evenings for their testimonial service, is the most convenient place for him to practice every day because it's located on the north side of downtown Brattleboro.

The First Congregational Church in West Brattleboro, where he plays every Sunday from November through April, is a few minutes farther away, on the other side of town. From April to September, he subs at one church or another every Sunday.

Therefore, it's quite organized of him to keep his music, his narrow Capezio organ shoes, and the all-important reading glasses in his music bag as he drives his circuit of churches, voice lessons, and rehearsals for whatever concert he is rehearsing for.

The other item Bill found today was his honey bear. (No, that is not me.)

He had taken his empty plastic honey bear to the Putney Food Co-op a week ago to refill it with honey. Then we went to Saturday brunch at Paul and Karen's and came home.

Bill had pawed through the back seat of my car and called Karen twice, looking for his honey bear. Finally, he called the Co-op, and yes, they had it sitting on the check-out counter with a "Paid" sticker on it.

I love it when Bill finds things—as he always does—whether it's the credit card lost for four months and then found in his bathrobe pocket or the notebook for his concert program lost for three weeks and then found on a cinder block beside the furnace. For me it's a practice in patience.

A GOOD DEED A DAY

I DO BELIEVE THAT BILL does a good deed every day. This only occurred to me recently as I accompanied him twice for walks in the snowy woods.

The first time, he was armed with his chainsaw; the second with my pruning saw. We crunched through the thinning icy snow for five minutes to arrive at our destination—two trees fallen over the ski trail. An eight-inch-diameter ash had taken an eight-inch dead pine with it when it fell.

Neighbor Connie had snowshoed out a few days before, when there was still enough snow to shoe on, and with her pruning saw lopped off enough of the dead pine's branches to reduce the double tree-death from a hurdle to a broad jump, though still impossible for senior citizens on cross-country skis.

Trees on top of snow hid whatever might have lain below, but the snow was rotten enough that Bill could kick his foot underneath the tree and then know where to saw down and where to saw up so his chain saw wouldn't get pinched. Five cuts and five four-foot logs later, the trail was clear. No more screeching to a halt on edge-less skis in the middle of what should be a comfortable downhill coast.

Two days later, we went for another walk in the woods with my pruning saw hanging from Bill's belt. This time we walked through the woods for fifteen minutes before reaching our destination—a sapling lying across the trail, weighted down by icy snow and thus too awkward and heavy to budge. A few strokes of the light-duty saw freed the sapling, and the brook trail, the most scenic trail on the eighty wooded acres of our neighborhood, was available for cross-country skiing—just in case we have any more snow this winter.

On Monday and Tuesday of this week, Bill's good deed had to do with the New England Coalition on Nuclear Pollution (NEC). On Monday, he spent the afternoon at the Vernon Town Clerk's office looking at the land records for the land the atomic plant now sits on. On Tuesday night, he spent two hours in Vernon at a boring Public Service Board meeting about the closing of the Vermont Yankee nuclear power plant. Whatever the chore, he usually spends a couple of afternoons a week volunteering at NEC.

On Sundays, you could say his good deed is providing piano and organ music, mini-concerts really, for whatever church he's playing for. And the same could be said of Wednesday nights, when he plays the organ for the Christian Science testimonials. On Thursdays, he goes to his Rotary Club meeting at noon. He loves the service aspect, volunteering at least once and often twice a month for various Rotary projects on Saturdays.

A good deed a day. That's one factor about healthy aging that I haven't read about.

TOGETHERNESS

Bill and I travel so that we can be together 24/7, or, more usually, 24/14—that is, a couple of weeks away from home, away from our routine. I love our routine at home, but our physical togetherness there is a bit thin. You'd think that two retired people would spend all their time together and become tired of each other, but we're each too busy for that.

I arise three hours before he does, and then at eight o'clock I walk to a neighbor's house for meditation with five other neighbors. By the time I return home at nine, Bill is sitting at the breakfast table, listening to NPR, and reading yesterday's newspaper. He spends an hour in the kitchen, preparing and eating his full breakfast. I sit down next to him for five or maybe ten minutes. Then I'm off—to the garden in the spring and summer, or to the computer in the chill of fall and winter. Most mornings I'm home, and he's home. I'm on the third floor; he's in his music studio in the basement. On Sunday mornings we both go to work.

We seldom eat lunch together. Our afternoons are busy in our own particular directions. For three evenings a week, I'm exercising at the circus school or teaching meditation classes. On Wednesday evenings, he plays organ for the Christian Science testimonials. This leaves us the weekend evenings together.

On Thursday morning at the breakfast table, Bill plans our weekend. On Friday night, we might go to a play. And he fits in three or four concerts each weekend for himself. My limit is one musical event per weekend, so Bill often goes by himself or with one of his five musical girlfriends—driving an hour north to "the Hop" at Dartmouth or an hour south to the Springfield Symphony or just half an hour to the Pioneer Valley Symphony in Greenfield, Massachusetts.

And the next week, it's pretty much the same thing.

So we plan a trip. In the motel room, I still wake up three hours earlier than he does and I hang out, waiting for him. Then we go to breakfast together, which Bill loves. I look at the breakfast menu and sigh. Who serves a vegan breakfast, anyway?

Our travel day starts at about ten o'clock, and then we're in the car together all day or taking a hike or seeing sights. We have lunch together and dinner together. Without a piano or his Roku, Bill comes to bed just half an hour later than I do, instead of at his usual hour. But by then my eyelids have drooped, and as soon as I feel the warmth of his body in bed, I fall asleep in about three breaths.

Togetherness.

SILENT SONATA

Bill comes to bed at eleven. I've been asleep for half an hour, but I wake up to pee in the hope that urgency won't wake me again for four or five hours.

When I come back to bed, I lie on my left side, away from Bill's reading light, which he soon turns off. He's been lying on his right side to read; now he turns onto his left side. In the spring, summer, or fall, it's too hot for tight spooning, so he just lays his right hand on my waist.

As he drops off, the fingers of his right hand begin to lightly play my skin as if it's a piano for a couple of minutes. Then I hear his heavy breathing and the silent sonata ceases.

FALLING IN LOVE WITH MABEL

I FELL IN LOVE WITH Mabel, Bill's mother, faster than I fell in love with Bill.

That Christmas Eve, I really did not want to go to New Jersey with Bill. We had been dating for two months, and he was driving down there to spend Christmas with his 84-year-old mother. I was so obstinate that I made him stop in front of the post office in Brattleboro. I got out of the car. "I am *not* going," I yelled and slammed the door of his blue Toyota Tercel station wagon.

He rolled down the passenger-side window and leaned over. "Cheryl," he said, "you can't stay here." He was right.

I sullenly got back into his car, and as he drove toward the interstate I broke into tears. "I want to spend Christmas at Connie's," I cried.

"Connie didn't invite you," he said gently.

By the time he drove onto the interstate, I had stopped sobbing. By the time we crossed the Massachusetts state line, we were talking as usual.

This was one of the things I loved about Bill. The first was that I felt at home with him, a feeling so comfortable that I didn't even recognize it as love. Second, even though I threw a temper tantrum every week, he still stuck around. "Oh, you're just afraid of getting close," he would say.

"No I'm not," I would reply. And he would smile.

Or, as he did that morning, he would gently and with thorough common sense respond to my fury, so that I really had no choice but to break into tears and calm down.

I had really tried to cut the falling-in-love bit as short as possible because I couldn't tolerate the anxiety. By age 41, I'd suffered—and I mean suffered the suffering—of a dozen broken relationships. I had no confidence at all that this relationship wouldn't meet the same fate within the next few months. Just five months earlier, he'd brought his wife and eleven-year-old daughter with him down to New Jersey to spend a week with his mother and go to the Seabright Beach Club, where Mabel had had a membership for 55 years. Now he was bringing me, his new girlfriend, to meet his mother.

Six hours later, we arrived in Little Silver, New Jersey, at his mother's condo in Cheshire Square. He called her Gammie; he never called her Mother anymore. I wasn't her grandchild, so I called her Mabel.

Mabel was only a year younger than my grandmother, Nonnie, who had died just a year previously. But Mabel wasn't like my crippled-up Nonnie in the slightest. First of all, Mabel sounded like Kathryn Hepburn, whom, I learned later, she actually knew. Mabel had been born with a silver spoon in her mouth and gone to Dobbs

Ferry, a girls' boarding school. After her months-long trip to Europe with all her friends in the mid-1920s, she married Anthony McKim.

They smoked and drank through their New York Social Register life for forty years till Tony died. Mabel was still smoking and drinking, something my own grandmother would never dream of doing. Mabel watched tennis and golf on TV—also something my Nonnie would never have considered. Mabel spent hours on the phone, gabbing with her friends about who was doing what. I had seldom seen my own grandmother on the telephone because phone calls were expensive.

After dinner—not cooked by Mabel, who spent very little time in the kitchen—Bill drove us to St. George's by the River, the Episcopal church he had attended as a child before he was sent off to St. Paul's, an Episcopal boarding school for boys in Concord, New Hampshire.

Bill dropped Mabel and me off at the entrance to the church while he went to park the car, and I offered her my arm as she negotiated the steps in the chill December darkness.

As we stood in the foyer, waiting for Bill, Mabel greeted an elderly woman and then introduced me. "This is my friend Cheryl."

I was immediately smitten. I'd known this woman for three hours, and already, I was her friend.

TRAVEL

SAN JUAN ISLAND

I'VE AMASSED A LOT of frequent-flyer miles and so I'm able to buy two one-way tickets to Seattle in September for 25,000 miles. Two tickets for 12,500 miles each was a good deal, but that means we have to fly according to United's schedule instead of ours.

We leave Hartford at 6:00 P.M. and arrive at SeaTac at midnight Pacific time. I've reserved a room at Motel 6 very near the airport. Very near the *other* side of the airport, as it turns out.

We walk into the barest of the bare Motel 6 rooms I have ever been in. Not only are there no pictures on the walls and no rugs on the fake-wood floor, the double-bed mattress is on a raised platform so that you can see completely underneath the bed. One chair at a table, two smallish bath towels (not four). One small bar of soap. No shampoo or body lotion to clutter up my luggage. Well, what do I expect for $59 a night?

"I'm going to wake you up when I wake up," I tell Bill. "Let's try to get a jump on the Seattle rush hour." If it were up to Bill, we wouldn't get started until 10:00 A.M. Then we wouldn't have a problem with traffic at all.

But I wake up early, and so it's five hours later when I trundle Bill into the white Corolla rental car. As soon as we reach I-5 and its five lanes of traffic rushing in each direction, we are smack in the middle of rush hour at 6:30 A.M.

Pretty soon, we face the decision to continue north on I-5 through downtown Seattle—always a slowly moving parking lot—or take I-205 through the cities just to the east that Seattle swallowed some decades ago. Now each interstate has six lanes headed in each direction.

Washingtonians tell me there is no advantage to 205, but I choose it anyway because it seems like it *should* be less crowded. Immediately it's clogged. That's when I realize that Bill is in the car with me, even though he's inert, reclining in the passenger seat. We can drive in the HOV lane, so we sail along at a pretty good clip, passing thousands, maybe tens of thousands of cars in our 20-mile bypass before 205 merges with I-5 again. Of course, there are slowdowns at times, and this is when I-the-driver try to instruct Bill-the-navigator in the use of Waze, a traffic app on my iPhone.

"Find the blue icon with the ghost on it. I think it's on the third page of apps."

Three minutes later, he's found it, and he now shows me the road ahead, which is punctuated with yellow balloons with black exclamation points. I try not to look. I'm keeping my eyes on the zillions of cars—a wide river of silver and red and blue salmon running to the sea.

We are headed to the sea ourselves: to the San Juan Islands above Puget Sound and within eyeshot of Canada. Can we make the 11:30 Washington State Ferry in Anacortes, which will convey us to Friday Harbor on San Juan Island itself?

At 11:00 A.M. we are in line for the 11:30 ferry, which has already arrived, and east-bound cars are driving off. The waiting lines are not too long, so we *will* be able to board instead of having to wait two hours for the next west-bound ferry. Bill doesn't even have time to go get a cup of coffee before our lane of cars starts moving.

Once our car is among those parked like sardines on the ferry, there is nothing to do but get out of the car, walk up the stairs to the lounge, and relax and enjoy our hour-and-a-half ride. The small cafeteria serves a small selection of fast food. I opt for chili; Bill for a sausage-egg-and-cheese muffin. We both lie down on the long, green Naugahyde bench seats, but I am unable to catch a wink, so we stare out the windows and watch various islands of the San Juans go by.

At one o'clock, we drive off the ferry into Friday Harbor, a little town with a few dozen boutique and souvenir stores and a couple of dozen restaurants.

Thanks to the map app on the iPhone, we head directly to a museum parking lot where we proceed to recline our seats and take a nap.

Twenty minutes later, I lazily come to consciousness, looking through the windshield at the overgrown hill that rises straight up in front of us. And then I focus on the brambles—blackberries! Big, juicy, really ripe blackberries. "Blackberries!" I moan to the still-supine Bill.

I've never been fond of the hard little blackberries I tug from the vines in the woods near my house, but these island berries fall right into our hands. They've soaked up a year of Pacific Northwest rain. Our fingers turn purple as we have our free lunch that consists entirely of blackberries.

We drive on to the bike rental shop, where we rent bicycles for the next three days. After checking in at the Olympic Lights B&B, we take our first spin on the bikes. We keep stopping along the road at the next bramble patch, and the next, and the next one after that.

We've traveled by plane, by car, by ferry, and by bicycle today, getting closer and closer to blackberries. We thought we were coming here to bicycle in the San Juan Islands, a different island every day, but it turns out that the bicycles are just a way to slow down enough to spot the blackberries growing on the side of every road and feast to our purple hands and hearts' content.

MICAH IN MEXICO

My 26-year-old nephew, Micah, went with us to Mexico in January. It was my first visit with him that was adult-to-adult, unmediated by parents, undistracted by his many guy friends. He was a perfect guest—good-natured, eager for good conversation, and grateful. He expressed no desire to break the mold of our old people's interests in museums, arts, markets, and food.

He did go hiking with Bill—four hours up and over a mountain pass in the Sierra Madre. And we all went bike-riding on the cobblestone streets of Oaxaca one night from 9:00 to 10:30 p.m. with forty other cyclists. Bill and I aren't old fogeys—yet.

But as Micah said on the last day, "What am I going to tell my friends?" No beach, no resort, no sunburn or even any suntan, no snorkeling, no tequila, no piña coladas, no pizza, no hamburgers, no night clubs, no parties, no TV, no movies, no Montezuma's revenge, no robberies. What kind of vacation was that?

Instead, he visited indigenous woodcarvers, potters, and weavers, explored Zapotec ruins and even attended a lecture about them. He spent hours in an archaeological museum, went to an art museum, toured the old opera house, and visited the home of Benito Juarez, who was the president of Mexico from 1858 to 1872. He walked through the courtyards of old colonial buildings and drank chocolate lattes for breakfast and a mid-afternoon pick-me-up. He listened to Uncle Bill play Chopin on a grand piano most afternoons at four o'clock. He looked at innumerable churches and got caught in an afternoon church service where he and Aunt Cheryl were the only people in attendance; they couldn't very well sneak out. He visited the homes of two of Aunt Cheryl's friends who live in Oaxaca and ate the fluffiest tamales ever. In fact, he ate Mexican food three meals a day and was in bed by ten at night.

What kind of vacation was that?

AUGUST VACATION

August is the month when it's time to relax and go on vacation, just in case you haven't been taking your summer seriously.

A few years ago, I developed my own personal theory of summer: Do something summery every day. Then you won't feel like you've missed out. You won't look around on August 1 and think, *August first already? Oh, no! Summer, glorious summer is almost over, and I still haven't had my summer vacation yet.*

What's your definition of summer vacation? Swimming in a pool, or a river, or a lake, or a pond? Some would say the ocean. Kayaking at sunrise or sunset or mid-afternoon with friends. Picnics and picnic food. Reading books. Reading a book a day or at least five a week. Getting a tan, not through sunbathing but simply from being outdoors. That is, *not* cocooned in the house with the virtual reality of words, texts, photos, and videos, because real reality is so much more sensorily pleasant. Sleeping outdoors in a tent and hearing, really hearing, the night.

Walking in the woods, hiking in the mountains, bicycling on back roads. Wearing shorts and tank tops every day. Waking up early with the first birdsong to enjoy the dawning of a new day. Going to as many plays, and Bill would say operas, as possible. Attending at least one, and sometimes three, plays or concerts in the park to which you bring your own picnic and share your goodies with the people around you. I go to one Farmers' Market every week, usually the one in Putney on Sundays around noon.

Yes, there's some gardening, but it's too hot to do very much. So harvesting is the main thing—taking the basket out to the garden and being surprised by what fills it up in just a few minutes.

Eating from the garden—kale salad, tomato sandwiches, cucumbers, summer squash, green beans. Stopping at the farm stand for three ears of corn every day. And berries! Berries are my favorite fruit. Eating a pint of raspberries every day in July—red or black. Blueberries every day in August and as long as they last in September. Watermelon. I now grind up a quarter of a watermelon every day or two and drink it. A summer guest recently said he hadn't eaten so much healthy food every day in years.

Watching fireflies on a late June night, lying in a hammock with your sweetie. Sitting on the deck at dusk watching the bats do a superb job of eating mosquitoes, of which there aren't any buzzing around. Sitting on the terrace at ten at night, with all the lights in the house turned off, watching the moon and the stars or the meteor shower in mid-August.

My prescription for summer is to do at least one of these things every afternoon. I take my summer vacation in daily two-hour chunks. It's a stay-cation because we already live in a summer vacation destination. Vermont: it's green here. Really, really, really green. Downright verdant. Verde Vermont.

August. Eat it. Feel it, taste it, touch it, see it while you can.

MY TENT

When I was 39, I lived in my tent for 150 nights. I moved almost every day, except when I was in Helena or Havre or Missoula. I could put up my green-and-white three-person Kelty tent, blow up my Thermarest, get my cooking gear out of the back of the truck, and be sitting at the picnic table with my IBM laptop—the very first, and therefore still-uncommon, laptop—in five minutes.

"Are you an outfitter?" the man in a neighboring campsite asked.

No, I told him—just practiced in the art of setting up camp. On the road from April 15 to November 15, 1987. And I can tell you, camping out on the Hi-Line of Montana in mid-October is too late in the season to be camping; nights are long in the north, and the wind sweeps down from Alberta like marauding Blackfoot Indians.

I loved my tent, my refuge. In the big towns, I would stay in a KOA. Billings, Montana, on the Yellowstone River, was the very first KOA Kampground in the country. In the mountains, I stayed in primitive National Forest campgrounds, sometimes with a pump, sometimes without water. Always with an outhouse. Out there in those nearly deserted campgrounds, I tried to set up camp near an elderly couple, usually in an RV, small or large.

Some late afternoons, I'd boil water on my one-burner camp stove and sit inside my tent on a towel and give myself a sponge bath with a quart of hot water. I loved those baths—so small, so efficient, so clean, so outdoors.

Just a zippered screen door separated me from the mice camping out for the night under my ground cloth, or the practically tame deer in Wallowa State Park, or a moose trotting by in Beaverhead National Forest.

I put 25,000 miles on that tent that year. When the zipper on the door stopped working, I took it to a camping store for repair and learned about zippers. Sometimes they just need a slight squeeze with a pair of pliers. Sometimes they need a new zipper pull.

In Boise, I bought a new rainfly when the old one began to tear and pull apart due to too much sun exposure. One night in Harlowton, very near the exact center of Montana, the wind blew the tent flat on top me as I lay there in my sleeping bag, and one of the tent poles snapped. Duct tape just didn't have the proper flexibility, so I had to get new legs for that Kelty.

I loved that tent, which lasted a few more years, into my new relationship with Bill.

"Let me help," he'd say while I pouffed the tent up in the pouring rain on the Olympic peninsula in the dark of ten o'clock at night.

"No thanks," I'd say. "I can do it in five minutes. If you help, it will take ten."

When the second rainfly ripped a few years later, it was time to retire the Kelty and move into a Eureka! Equinox. Of which there were three over the course of a dozen years. And now my summer home is an REI Hobitat—a tent that looks like a hobbit home—a five-foot tall dome with a round screen door. Even after thirty years, I still love to set up my tent in a tribe of tents when I go camping with my neighbors on Lake Champlain.

My home away from home.

PACK RIVER STORE

I go to Sandpoint, Idaho, every September to visit my sister and her two adult sons. Sandpoint is a beautiful town of 7,500 people in the Idaho panhandle, an hour south of the Canadian border, one hour east of Washington state, and one hour west of Montana. It sits on a spit of sand on Lake Pend Oreille, just north of its smaller twin, Lake Coeur d'Alene.

The Monarch Mountains come right down to the edges of this 44-mile-long glacially-formed lake. Multimillion-dollar homes dot the shores of Lake Pend Oreille, and a fair number of recognizable celebrities as well as highly-paid corporate executives have their second, third, or fourth home here.

The little town has enough women's clothing shops to keep a female tourist busy for an entire afternoon. Three home décor stores and a couple of art galleries offer a chance to cleanse the shopping palate. When it's time to eat, you can choose from a dozen trendy restaurants, another dozen ethnic restaurants, and a handful of pubs. Sandpoint has twelve real estate offices, nine banks, and a handful of investment offices. The Chamber of Commerce puts out a glossy 130-page magazine twice a year, filled with interesting stories about Sandpoint.

Two hometown hardware stores and one hometown drugstore give Sandpoint a quaint, small-town feel. Cars really do stop for you when you want to walk across the street.

Rand-McNally calls Sandpoint "the Most Beautiful Small Town in America." *Sunset Magazine* names Sandpoint as "the Best Small Town in the West." From December through March, it's one of the Best Ski Towns, too, thanks to nearby Schweitzer Mountain. The fact that there's continual two- or three-foot snow cover in the forests around the town means that moose tend to wander down the conveniently plowed streets, down the plowed highways, and down both the east-west and north-south railroad tracks that cross in Sandpoint, which has Idaho's only Amtrak station. There's a lot of snow, and there are a lot of train-killed moose in the snowbanks beside the tracks.

Two miles north of downtown Sandpoint, the town of Ponderay (pronounced the same as Pend Oreille) has the big-box stores and supermarkets that serve the area. The population of Ponderay is 1,117, and there are probably about that many parking spaces in the various shopping plazas that are home to more than 170 businesses.

My sister's Jaguar with Idaho plates purrs along the streets and roads in the company of out-of-state BMWs and the occasional Maserati or Tesla. The locals drive Subarus.

It's fun shopping and eating in downtown Sandpoint, but I like to go to the Pack River Store.

Drive eight miles east out of town, toward the

Montana border. Turn north on the Pack River Road, past a non-functioning golf course surrounded by large new summer homes. Then turn east on Rapid Lightning. There, in the middle of nowhere, on the bank of the shallow and sandy Pack River, sits the Pack River Store with its single gas pump.

Pickup trucks constantly drive in and out of here, most of them beat-up and rattling, with bumper stickers that say *Wolves: Smoke a Pack a Day* or *Buck Ofama* or *Kill 'em All. Let God Sort Them Out*. Their drivers are here every day after work to pick up an eighteen-pack of the cheapest beer—Pabst, Hamms, or Natural Light—along with a pack of Pall Malls or Kools or a tin of Copenhagen Long Cut chew and maybe a pack of rolling papers.

Around the side of the store are the laundromat and showers and propane for those independent folks who live off the grid and whose bumper stickers say *I Get My Energy from the Sun* or *Coexist*. A few of these liberals have wolves as pets.

I go to the Pack River Store for the breakfast burritos, the baked goods, or the nightly specials of pork tenderloin or Salisbury steak. The breakfast pizza of biscuit dough and layers of sausage gravy, eggs, and cheese is also tasty. Or just choose something delicious from the deli case.

I watch any number of well-worn blue jeans, none clean or pressed, walk in and out of the swinging screen door that bangs behind each customer. Hair is usually a bit long over the ears of the men and halfway down the back of the woman. All the faces are sun-worn. Baseball caps, some of them in camo, are the predominant headgear. A few hundred workboots every day long ago scuffed off any varnish that may have once been on the floor and sanded it down to dirt-brown.

The clientele pays mostly in cash, and they're all well known to Arlene, the proprietor. Visitors like me use credit cards. In the summer, the tourists are usually bicycling or kayaking by or coming in for a last-minute bottle of wine, of which Arlene has a surprisingly good selection.

But mostly these Pack River people are the carpenters, the plumbers, and the stonemasons who build those beautiful custom houses on the lake. These are the metal and wood artisans who customize each house into a work of art. These are the beef or buffalo ranchers and the alpaca or lamb farmers, who spin and dye the wool that can be found at the very good Farmers' Market. These are the loggers who haul red fir and the strong western larch to the local sawmills. These are the elk hunters and the kokanee fisherman and the outfitter guides who patch together a living from picking up whatever seasonal work they can find. These are the wounded vets who live like hermits in ramshackle trailers with a wood stove slapped in, and Arlene is their entire social contact for the day or for the week.

On Friday evening, as we finish our Salisbury steak dinners at the round oak table at the Pack River Store, I tell my sister, "*Now* I feel like I've really been to Idaho."

CHERYL'S MEMORIES

RACING

"Sis. Run down and get the paper for me," Dad would say when he came home from the horse barn, five miles away.

"I don't want to," I'd reply as I shuffled around the living room.

The *Greenfield Reporter* was thrown out of the window of a moving car every evening at about five, and it would land somewhere in the half acre of the front yard, closer to state road 209 than to our house. It was only a hundred feet away, but I was a sickly child with severe asthma, sometimes athletically induced asthma. About half my young life was spent either coming down with an asthma attack or getting over one. For the other half of my life I could jump rope and play tag, though sometimes it did cause me to wheeze.

"I'll time you," Dad would say and reach into his pocket to pull out his stopwatch, the stopwatch he timed his trotters and pacers with. I could pretend I was a horse and see how fast I could run. I'd walk to the front door.

"Ready. Set. Go!" Dad would say, and I'd run down to get the paper and run back again. I'd see him check his watch and smile. "Twenty-five seconds!"

I was huffing and puffing and happy as I handed him the thin, rolled-up newspaper with a green rubber band around it. All the doorknobs in our house were braceleted with dozens of green rubber bands. Mother used one for my ponytail every morning.

Dad would settle into his black Naugahyde recliner with the black-and-white upholstery on the back and the seat while I was still breathing hard. Racing always seemed as if it would be so much fun.

Who's going to be first into the car? Who's going to be last? Last was never good because Dad would get mad at whoever was last, usually Mom.

Who's going to be there when Dad brought candy home, once every week or two? A box of chocolate-covered cherries, maybe, or a bag of Red Hots. If you were last, there wouldn't be any left for you. Last was not good. Fast was good.

I got dressed fast in the morning after Dad turned on the overhead light at 6:30 A.M. I tried to get into the bathroom first. And it was good to be fast in our one and only bathroom; otherwise someone would be complaining in the hallway. And complaining might bring Dad on the rampage.

It was good to be first in the kitchen where Dad was baking Pillsbury biscuits and frying bacon or sausage. If Mom was boiling oatmeal, there was no need to hurry.

Put on jacket and scarf quickly—or Dad might say, "Make it snappy." And it was very good to be early for the school bus. I would stand at the end of our driveway for five or ten minutes in my thin, cotton-plaid dress, crouching down so that the skirt tented over my bare legs and felt warmer than the winter air.

"Don't make the school bus wait on you," Dad said. His dad had driven a school hack during the Great Depression, and I bet he had a short temper, too.

I liked the speed-reading contests at school, the ciphering matches, and the spelling bees. I often won because I was quick and bright.

I learned to be fast, work fast, do things efficiently. I could save time, a second here or there, by putting things in order. Early was good. Faster was better. I was always racing against the clock, trying to beat the clock when we watched game shows on TV and shouted out answers.

It didn't matter if you left a mess behind you. Wash those supper dishes fast so you could go watch TV in the living room with everyone else.

Get ready for bed fast. Then go to bed and go fast asleep, or else whisper quietly to my sister in our double bed.

I could do anything fast—such as my homework, whether reading or math. I could sew fast, eat fast, go to the bathroom fast, and even sing fast. Slow was slowpoke. Slow was my brother Paul, who couldn't read. Dad yelled at him. Slow would never win the race.

I wanted to win. Win my dad's approval and affection.

PLAYING COLLEGE

WHEN I WAS IN fifth grade, I played college outdoors with my sister Dona and the neighbor girl Karol. They quickly tired of it, but for fifteen or twenty minutes, we each had a stack of books and went to imaginary classrooms around the yard—under the maple, in the playhouse, at the swing set. After a few minutes, it was time to change and go to another class. We talked briefly between classes and told each other which class we were going to next. After about three classes, the others had had enough of this lonely game, so we'd switch to dress-ups or my sister's favorite game, ranch, when she could wear her cowgirl outfit.

In the 1950s, aspiring cowgirls watched Dale Evans and Roy Rogers on TV on Saturday afternoons. Like Dale, my cowgirl sister wore a skirt with a fringed hem and a vest with fringe. Dale's hat was probably buckskin. Our black-and-white TV just showed a shade of gray, but Dona wore a red cowgirl hat. She didn't have any cowgirl boots; we were all running around barefoot in our one-acre yard.

We'd each name our ranch—the Circle K for Karol, the lazy D for Dona, the Bar C for Cheryl. While Dona rode her hobbyhorse or lined up the plastic horses in her horse collection, I'd keep the books on how many cows I had and how many calves, and how many were going on a cattle drive.

Fifty-five years later, you could say I'm still playing the same game of college, except that the distances are farther apart. On Wednesday morning I drive to a meditation group, where we are learning a new chant. Then I get into my iron pony and drive to my new aerial yoga class at the circus school, where I learn to do yoga using fabric as a prop. After shivasana in the cocoon of fabric, I hop back into my chariot and drive to my writing group, another sort of class.

When I was ten, I already knew I'd be a lifelong learner, even though I'd never heard that term. And keeping track of my imaginary cattle ranch turned into bookkeeping for companies and organizations.

My sister gave up her love of horses at age thirteen after being stepped on and kicked too many times by Dad's Standardbred horses, but she did eventually live on a hundred-acre ranch in the West and felt utterly at home there, even though the only animals were her husband's English setters and her own cat. She always did love the cats at the horse barn, and her wrists and arms were usually raked with scratches.

While we girls were playing our games with each other, our five-year-old brother, Paul, was running his cars and trucks and tractors around in the ten-foot-square sand pile. That turned out to be his life's work—bulldozers and backhoes, carving roads into fields and digging ditches for waterlines and sewers. Even in his retirement, he still has a few pieces of heavy equipment, and he quarries lithified sand—a beautiful and rare Hoosier sandstone—that landscapers love for its golden, pink, and white tones.

His friend in the sand pile—Danny, Karol's younger brother—was killed at age fifty when his giant motorcycle was blown off the road on a very windy day.

Our youngest brother, Beau, collected seeds and planted trees at age five. Although he studied forestry at Purdue, he left that calling to follow Jesus. Still, he can't help but plant seeds and trees whenever he moves to a new house. I could call him Beau Redbudseed or Beau Oak for the many acorns he gathers, germinates, and plants every fall.

The summer after seventh grade, I decorated a shed-*cum*-playhouse at Dad's horse barn, five miles away from home. Just fixing up the playhouse was enough; I didn't actually play in it. I painted the old shed in gray and pink. And what do you know? Twenty years later I moved into my own gray house with barn-board siding—and yes, I painted the trim pink.

Who needs to ask a child what they're going to be when they grow up? Just watch them play. Their life's work is presaged in their play.

THE DIFFERENCE BETWEEN MEN AND WOMEN

What's the difference between men and women? This is what I thought when I was ten years old in 1958:

- Men are the bosses.
- Women have the stupid jobs.
- People listen to men.
- They don't listen to women.
- In couples, the woman keeps her eye on the man. The man is in the lead, so he's not looking at the woman.
- Men watch sports on TV.
- Women stay in the kitchen and talk about recipes and babies.
- Men get to decide things.
- Women nod.
- Men are gruff.
- Women are beautiful.
- Men go to work.
- Women stay home.
- Men have money.
- Women have to beg for money. Then they spend it.

What's a girl to do when she doesn't want to be like her mother, her grandmothers, or her aunts? What's a girl to do when she's the smartest person in her class?

I was so proud of my cousins Sharon and Nancy, who were five years older than I was. They were both cheerleaders in high school. Then they graduated, worked as secretaries, got married, and had babies when they were twenty.

Wait a minute. If that's what it means to be a woman, then I'm not doing that.

But as a freshman in my very small, rural high school, the only elective I could take was home economics. I rolled my eyes and put up with one more year; I'd already had two years of home ec in junior high. One more year of home ec with Miss Shepherd. She wasn't even a Missus. And what kind of home did she have, anyway? I think she lived with her mother.

I started reading. No. I was already an avid reader. I started reading the classics and got a strong impression of what Victorian women were like: quiet, poor governesses, in love with unattainable men. But they worked hard and were true to themselves, and the men eventually asked for their hands in marriage. I actually tried this approach to being a woman for several years. I kept expecting that some man would notice my homemaking skills and choose me. No luck.

My beautiful mother trained my sister and me in beauty and sewing our own wardrobes. We learned cooking by osmosis and were prepared to keep our own homes and decorate them beautifully. My sister was beautiful, and, I understand now, had pheromones. She got married at age twenty and embarked on the life of a homemaker.

But makeup and good-looking clothes could not disguise my essential nerdiness. Besides, I wanted to travel the world and broaden my horizons.

I really had no idea that women were supposed to be soft and loving and supportive. I didn't know that women were supposed to be emotional and feeling-ful. I was thoughtful, not feeling-ful. I was analytical, not soft and mushy. I was helpful, but not outwardly loving. I was a problem-solver, not a conversationalist. I was quiet and stand-offish, not a flirter.

When I was a senior in high school, the principal called me into his office to discuss the results of my aptitude test. I would be a good researcher or a nuclear engineer, he said. My score was high in math and science. And he informed me, sounding as if he were puzzled, that I had scored higher on masculine than feminine traits.

I didn't really understand what he was talking about. It would take another eight years before I decided that, as a woman, I was really quite inept.

I didn't start dating until I was twenty, and I could not understand why my girlfriends would sacrifice their futures for the sake of a boyfriend-cum-husband. Babies were so boring. I worked at a day-care center for Navajo migrant children when I was 22 and didn't bond with a single child there. When I was 25, all of a sudden all my girlfriends were coupled. I just couldn't seem to make that happen in my own life. And if their relationship broke up, it only took them a few weeks or months to fall in love again. I was in love at age 23 and again at age 35. Those guys in between were nice enough, but definitely not "the one." I tried being the obsequious girlfriend, constantly giving in to the man and praising him, but that felt disingenuous. I simply felt like a failure as a woman until life began at 40.

How it all unraveled, I cannot truly say. Was it the two and a half years of Deep Feeling therapy, where I worked through my fury at men? The Rolfing body work to ease the habitual armor out of my body? The months of "loving myself as I am" meditation?

At age 40, when I met Bill, I barely took the time to fall in love with him; it was more like coming home to myself. With him, I finally relaxed into being bossy, opinionated, judgmental, self-reliant, independent, and interdependent. And we could laugh about it all, together. I could be smart without fear of outsmarting the man. I could speak my truth. I could stop pretending to be feminine. I could drive my truck, use my chain saw, paint the house, exterior and interior. And, with my man, I could consistently pleasure myself to orgasm instead of vicariously hitchhiking on his pleasure.

Man-woman or woman-man really makes no difference. I simply came home to myself.

TREASURER

When I was in fifth grade, my friend Beth and I formed our own club, and I was the treasurer.

That's it. End of story. Even though I tried mightily to avoid that story in favor of some other more interesting, more glamorous story.

Sixty years later, I'm still the treasurer of a tiny club—the Master Gardeners of Windham County. We have $600 in our checking account and give a $200 scholarship to the Master Gardener training every year.

Although I haven't been the treasurer of the meditation center for six years, I recently volunteered to support the new treasurer by being on the Finance Committee.

I was treasurer of my junior class, treasurer of the Methodist Youth Fellowship (MYF) at the Willow Branch church I grew up in, and treasurer of the county MYF. I declined the nomination to be the treasurer of my senior class. I regret that refusal now, but that denial was the beginning of my attempt to push away from destiny in favor of the Drama Club, the school newspaper, the yearbook staff, and the committees for the Junior and then Senior Prom. Anything but the treasurer's job. Please.

During summers in our college years, my dad put my sister and me to work in his office, where we learned bookkeeping—a skill I never wanted, though later I could always find a job as a bookkeeper. Employers trusted me.

In my twenties, I tried other jobs, wanted other jobs—cross-cultural communications trainer, administrator and then director of human services agencies. But if my income got thin, I'd patch together two or three bookkeeping jobs. When I was 27, a boyfriend advised me to go into business for myself as a bookkeeper, but I wanted to be the director of a human services agency.

In my thirties, I wanted to be a computer programmer, but to tide me over, I got a job as a bookkeeper for a high-tech company. I started taking accounting courses, but, one course away from a second bachelor's degree, I couldn't stomach the thought of being a CPA. I worked my way up to controller of a construction company, but I wanted to be a psychotherapist.

I wrote a history book and then, when the grant that supported my writing ran out, I got a job as a financial consultant, helping little companies with their bookkeeping.

I went back to school for a master's in counseling. I was asked to be on the board of hospice . . . and by the way, would I take on the treasurer's duties? I handed that responsibility over after a year. Push away, push away. I want to be a writer. And now I'm the treasurer of four little groups.

Just bite the bullet, Cheryl. Say "yes" to destiny. Those other things you wanted have come and gone, and you still think balancing your checkbooks is a fine way to relax before going to bed.

BOOKKEEPING

When I was seventeen, I wasn't much of a job-hunter. Previously, I had spent my summer vacations lying on the sofa reading a book a day. Besides, there weren't too many jobs in the corn and soybean fields where I lived.

My dad found my first job for me. He was on the Indiana State Fair Board, and he knew Joe O'Brien, who ran the Racing Office. Five of us, sixteen- and seventeen-year-old girls, typed up letters with two carbon copies on Smith-Corona and Royal typewriters. "Enclosed please find two tickets for the race on September 2." We kept track of every seat in the grandstand and bleachers for ten days of horse and car races.

The next summer, I went to work for Dad. His secretary, Elise, showed me how to calculate and write payroll checks. The very next week she resigned, so I was mostly alone in the tiny two-bedroom house that was Dad's office across the street from Sleepy Hollow, a subdivision he was selling lots in, near Castleton.

He interviewed women the next week and hired the hottest young mother—Sue, a buxom platinum blonde with three children in grade school and a cheerful, sociable personality. Sue showed me how to make journal entries, and thus I began to learn double-entry bookkeeping.

By the following summer, 1967, Dad had moved his office to Carmel. Besides Sue as secretary, he now had a full-time bookkeeper—Pat Emmert. My sister Dona and I both learned to run the ten-key calculator by touch with the right hand, while keeping the left index finger on long columns of our hand-written numbers. We learned how to record checks in the over-sized ledger and then balance the books at the end of the month, and how to reconcile bank statements. Our bookkeeping jobs continued for two more summers.

When I was in high school, I had looked down my nose at the girls in the commercial track who took typing, bookkeeping, shorthand, and business math. Yes, of course I took typing because I could see how typing seventy words per minute would be useful for typing up theme papers in college. But bookkeeping? I never wanted to learn bookkeeping; I didn't like boring old arithmetic.

Algebra was really interesting, and I went to regional algebra contests as a freshman and again as a junior. But bookkeeping? Yech. Nevertheless, my classmates elected me as their junior class treasurer, and I did an excellent job of keeping track of the money—from our sales of newspapers, pencils, magazines, candy, and Christmas cards—so that we could take our senior class trip to Washington, D.C.

In between my bachelor's degree in 1970 and my master's degree in 1972, I got a job as a bookkeeper while

I lived in Hawai'i for six months. And after my master's degree, I had two part-time bookkeeping jobs, one part-time typing job, and a temporary job as a cross-cultural trainer at the same time.

I finally found a job as an administrator, and I whizzed through the preparation of monthly financial reports and annual budgets for my little organization. In 1982, when I moved to Portland, Oregon, at the age of 34, the first thing I did was get a job as a bookkeeper. Oh, what the heck. I started taking nighttime accounting classes at Portland Community College and then at Portland State University until I was three credit hours short of an accounting degree. But I really did not want to become a Certified Public Accountant.

I became the financial director of a high-tech company, and then the controller of a construction company, and then the government finance director of World Learning, where I managed several million dollars in grants. I took a break to follow my passion and write a book. But then, to support myself, I got a job as a financial consultant, helping little companies set up their bookkeeping systems.

I never wanted to be a bookkeeper, but bookkeeping is one of the most useful skills I have.

CHERYL (ALSO)

IN A WRITING WORKSHOP on "Light and Darkness" last December, I met a person named Cheryl, whom I automatically disliked. Oh, I have met my opposites before, but this was the darkest shadow I have encountered in a long time.

Usually I get a kick out of saying, "Hi, Cheryl," and hearing the echo, "Hi, Cheryl." I say it to the tall Cheryl; I am short. I say it to the Cheryl who weighs twice as much as I do. I say it to the young bank teller, who surprises me by having my now old-fashioned name.

The Cheryl in the writing group was tall and heavyset, and she walked with a cane. Her shoulder-length hair was pure white. Mine still looks brown, though I'm sort of hiding the gray in the center.

No, the thing about this Cheryl that I could not swallow was that she was a woman-man.

She was built like a 220-pound man; her voice was deep. In the group, she spoke first or early, as a man will do. In fact, I once knew a man, two years older than I, named Cheryl, but he spelled it Sherrell. His parents named him just as the name was coming into popularity in the 1940s, but then Cheryl quickly became unequivocally a woman's name. I sat in my writing workshop circle, wondering what this Cheryl's name had been originally.

Just which letter of the LGBTIQ she was, I couldn't say. Was she a he becoming a she? A she becoming a he? An L? A B? Or a T of some sort, if not of gender, then of clothing? I did admire her narrow shoes, which I much preferred to the men's shoes that I find heavy and clunky. Was this Cheryl totally comfortable on the outer fringes of she-ness?

My sweetie tells me I am the man and he is the woman in our relationship. I am the boss, the problem-solver, the decision-maker, even the moneybag. He is the relational one, the social one, the dithering one. He is the one who cries easily, and he loves to receive flowers. Ever since I took an aptitude test in high school and scored high in engineering and research, I've wondered just what kind of man-woman I am.

In all our talk of light and darkness at that writing workshop, we also spoke of shadow. And there she was, sitting directly across the circle from me.

SOCIAL ANXIETY

I'M TEACHING A CLASS called Calming Your Anxious Mind. Although I don't consider myself an anxious person, and am, in fact, almost worry-free, I do have some little social anxieties hiding in the wings, so well camouflaged under some ego defenses as to be nearly invisible.

I'm scared of people. My jaw drops when I hear our twelve-year-old granddaughter say, "I *love* people." That's her way of expressing gratitude for a bottle of water from a passing hiker when we were parched while climbing Mt. Monadnock.

I am terrified to ask for what I want or need, while Bill doesn't think twice about stating his needs and even expecting that they will somehow be met by the other person.

My father belonged to the don't-spoil-them school, so early on, I knew better than to ask for what I needed or wanted. My method of self-soothing was to become self-reliant. Thus, I am an excellent problem-solver, partly because I can't tolerate the anxiety of uncertainty, of not-knowing. When anxiety begins to rear its head, I immediately and unconsciously jump to problem-solving. I also can't tolerate the anxiety of seeing other people hurting, for instance, or seeing them anxious about what's going to happen next.

Bill had a nurse in his nursery, and let's just assume that she doted on him. He grew up with a cook in the kitchen, and a maid, and even a laundress, named Marcelini Brown, who picked up and delivered the laundry every Thursday. He doesn't hesitate to ask for anything, even difficult things. He feels comfortable with being helpless, because the help will help him. That's their job.

Me? I'm busy trying to figure out how to do it myself. I've recently tweaked one of my loving-kindness phrases: *May I feel safe asking for what I need.*

Yes, there's a trill of anxiety galloping back and forth across my chest, above my heart. *What if Daddy gets mad and spanks me?* I'm 66 years old, and my father has been dead for sixteen years, but his frown is still alive in my body.

So I practice asking: asking store clerks where something is, asking directions, asking questions, even asking questions that I think are stupid. I practice, practice, practice not-knowing in an effort to calm the subtly anxious body-mind.

JUNGIAN ANALYSIS

I started Jungian dream analysis in 1979, when I was 31, sort of by accident. My boyfriend recommended the nearby analyst to me because I wondered about the vivid dreams I sometimes had.

I would dream that a man was in bed with me even though I was sleeping alone. I could feel his body pressing up against me, feel the texture of his wool pants. But my voice was paralyzed. I couldn't ask who he was. And my body was paralyzed by sleep; I couldn't turn over to see who he was. Sometimes, I would hear him coming up the stairs. I wanted to shout, but could not.

As it turned out, the analyst never did answer my question about the meaning of those terrifically realistic hypnogogic dreams, but I kept writing down my nightly dreams and taking in one a week for him to analyze. This went on for two and a half years. My dreams slowly changed from two men chasing me to one man chasing me and one man helping me until finally the bad guys disappeared from my dreams altogether. Sometimes the man helping me out of sticky situations was a black man.

I started reading the basic books by Carl Jung, and one by one I added other Jungians to my collection:

Maria Louisa von Franz, Helen Luke, Robert Johnson, Esther Harding.

In 1982, I moved from Vermont to Portland, Oregon, and looked for a Jungian analyst there. The woman I wanted was completely booked, so I settled for a Jungian women's group, which was rather unsatisfying. I attended the monthly meetings of the Portland Friends of Carl Jung and heard fascinating lectures by many visiting Jungians.

With no Jungian analysts available to me, I finally tried another kind of therapy called Deep Feeling, which turned out to be a life-changing experience. My seething anger, particularly toward men, was released like steam from a boiler.

All through the 1980s I kept reading Jungian books. I returned to Vermont in 1985, and the next summer I attended a weeklong Jungian workshop in New York City. In 1990, I applied to the Boston Jung Institute, but I was rejected. I tried going back to the local analyst, but he wanted an open-ended commitment of years; I was thinking a couple of months. He sent me to an analyst in Boston, and I drove there every two weeks for nine months, until I tired of hearing her talk so much. I switched to an analyst in Peterborough, New Hampshire, about an hour away from home.

My vanity license plate said META4 because I so love the meaning of metaphor in daily life. Dream analysis honed my skill with metaphoric dream images. When my neighbors' stove broke down, I wondered about the heat in their marriage. (They separated a few months later.)

In 1991, I went to Antioch New England for a master's degree in counseling, but I didn't take the Jungian concentration because it was taught by my former analyst, and changing roles with him just felt too complicated.

For my graduation present to myself, in 1993, I went to a two-week summer program at the Jung Institute in Küsnacht, Switzerland, just outside Zurich, where Carl Jung had lived and worked. There I saw Bonnie Arendt, a woman from my Portland Jungian women's group, whom I hadn't seen in ten years.

I looked and looked at all that book candy in the Institute bookstore. I took copious notes from each fascinating presenter. And I thought long and hard about becoming a Jungian analyst.

When I came home, I divided a sheet of paper into two columns: Advantages and Disadvantages. There was one advantage: to be saturated in Jungian thought. And there were ten disadvantages. If I was going to train in Switzerland, I would need to begin immediately in order to do my practicum before I turned fifty, Switzerland's upper age limit on foreigners working in their country.

On the basis of that single sheet of paper, I gave up. I gave up my Jungian analyst. I gave up my dream of becoming a Jungian analyst. I gave away my collection of a hundred Jungian books.

And my love affair with Carl Jung was over.

FAMILY MEETINGS

When I was 36 and living in Portland, Oregon, I dated a financial planner. Actually, he was a carpenter in a suit, and I was a back-to-the-lander in a suit. After dropping out and tuning in during our twenties, along with so many in our baby-boomer generation of flower children, we were now trying to grow up and become yuppies.* We, who hadn't trusted anyone over thirty, were now over thirty ourselves and still not settled into adulthood. We had both supported ourselves since college; we both owned houses, which we rented out to other people so we could live in the city of Portland where the jobs and dates with the opposite sex were. Yet, at the onset of middle age, we were both still trying to figure out what we wanted to be when we grew up.

Harlan was four days older than I was, and, as it turned out, suits were not a good fit for either one of us. But despite our twinness, we weren't a good fit for each other, either.

My financial planner boyfriend set up my first IRA. Individual Retirement Accounts were ten years old, but I

---

* Yuppie comes from the acronym for "Young Urban Professionals," the next generation after hippies (who were "hip").

had never heard of them until 1984. Prior to our becoming yuppies, neither of us had earned enough to even think about saving for retirement.

Harlan was the caboose in his family; his two siblings were eight and ten years older than he was. His father was in his late seventies and of uncertain health. We talked generally of inheritance, and Harlan suggested that I start with an inventory of my own father's holdings. Then we broke up.

If I had really wanted to be upwardly mobile, I would have moved back to Indiana and gone to work for my father. He had been fishing for me for years, dangling the bait of money. "Come back and work for me, Sis," he would say. "You'll be rich." But I was a human services type, bent on saving the world, not on saving money.

The bait for his generation, who came of age during the Great Depression and then went off to fight World War II, had been money, and he was a rags-to-riches man. He and three of his four brothers had become postwar entrepreneurs who rode the booming economy into the middle class. Then, flying by the seat of his pants, Dad leveraged his way into a still higher income bracket.

By age 67, he had a construction company, a land development company, a shopping center, a water utility, and various partnerships with his cronies, owning this or that parcel of soon-to-be commercial land. He spent his afternoons with the love of his life—his Standardbred horses, a hobby he could now afford.

I knew my father had debts—a couple million dollars of bank loans. In the mid-1980s, prime interest rates were just coming down from 19, 18, 17 percent, and he paid 3 percent above that. What would happen if Dad had a heart attack and dropped dead? He had a short temper. I could easily imagine him having a heart attack during one of his temper tantrums, or maybe, while he was jogging his horses, he would fall backwards off his sulky onto the racetrack, dead.

And then what? Then my sister and two brothers and I would owe $2 million to the banks. Two years earlier, I had been receiving unemployment compensation. Working in human services, I had never made more than $12,000 a year in my life. I was in no shape at all to inherit acres of flat farmland and a mountain of debt from my consistently cash-poor father, who was maybe 5 percent liquid.

I spent the Christmas following my breakup with Harlan, a couple of weeks after we had turned 37, with my sister Dona, age 35, who lived in Washington state. We planned a spring trip to Indiana with two agenda items: we would have a family meeting with our two younger brothers in order to begin taking an inventory of Dad's holdings, and we would meet with a counselor in order to plan an intervention for our alcoholic mother, who carried the shadow side of Dad's rise from rags to riches. Dona and I wrote up an agenda for our family meeting, as we titled the proposed meeting with our brothers. I called and made an appointment with an alcohol counselor in Indianapolis for the first week of April.

To atone for my ill-fitting yuppie career in accounting, I had taken a year-long counseling course at Lutheran

Family Services. There I had met an alcohol counselor who told me about interventions.

So, in April 1985, Dona and I flew to Indianapolis. We were met at the airport by our thirty-year-old brother Beau, the youngest of us, with the fantastic news that our parents were getting divorced. That love-hate relationship would finally, finally come to the end that we'd all been waiting, waiting, waiting for.

Beau had flown up from Florida, leaving his pregnant wife at home with their almost-two-year-old son. As the youngest, Beau was the mascot of our family. When we were growing up, he had been Dona's and my pet, to whom we taught every board game and card game we knew—Clue, Sorry!, rummy, euchre. At age five Beau could beat us at the interminable games of Monopoly that lasted for most of a weekend. He was cute and talkative and kept everyone in a good mood.

Our brother Paul, number three, was, predictably in a dysfunctional family, the lost child. While Dona, Beau, and I had fled to the corners of the country, putting as much distance as possible between ourselves and our parents, Paul had plodded on, continuing to work for Dad, as he had since Dad first put him on a tractor at age five. Paul had become an alcoholic, and was now, at age 33, on Antabuse. He had four children and was in his third marriage. He showed up when he wanted to and dropped out of sight otherwise.

As the oldest, I was the hero who was trying, and had always tried, to save the family. This visit was to be the keystone of that effort.

Dona, in the number-two position, should have been the scapegoat. She had been a mischievous and beautiful little girl. As a teenager, she was the one most likely to push the limits, though she didn't push very far. Her escape from the scapegoat role was to get married at age twenty.

So I had inherited the scapegoat role, which Beau referred to as me being the lightning-rod. I would say something innocuous, and Dad would suddenly become furious. Dad's lightning storm would pass as quickly as it came, and I was left feeling a bit dazed and definitely not saying another word.

Growing up, Dona and I had fought like cat and dog, but the instant we were both in college we had become good friends.

Beau drove us from the airport to Mom and Dad's farmhouse on 146th Street in Carmel. The next morning, Dona, Paul, Beau, and I began our day-long family meeting at The Office.

Dona and I had worked at The Office every summer while we were in college, so we felt at home there. We had learned bookkeeping, a skill neither one of us wanted, but which would be the best skill either one of us would ever have. Dad's bookkeeper, Pat, had trained us, and now, eighteen years later, she still worked at The Office with ten sets of company ledgers. Jeff, the new accountant, just out of college, had been at The Office for less than a year and seemed an unlikely accountant personality. He spent time chatting with the women in the front office and planning office parties—at least one a month.

At this first family meeting, we had asked Pat and Jeff to simply walk us through Dad's various companies: Keystone Square Shopping Center, Hamilton Western Utilities, Wilfong Construction, Fine Builders, R. L. Wilfong Land Corporation, Westfield Investment Company, Fineberg-Wilfong joint venture, and Cool Creek Partnership.

Dad was both happy that we were taking an interest in his accomplishments and furious that we were acting like gold-diggers and perhaps even wishing for his death. He was frustrated when neither of us brighter ones—Beau or I—would bite on the money-baited hook he kept dangling. Dona was dismissed as a possibility because "she's married."

Before the birth of his first son, in May 1983, and lured by the prospects of nepotism, Beau had left his UPS job in Florida to come back to Indiana and work for Dad. Beau and his wife lived in the apartment in the farmhouse where Mom and Dad lived.

Dad had reneged on the amount he had agreed to pay Beau, and although Dad had yearned to have one of his children get to know the business, he retained all the power and control himself. So Beau had responsibility but no authority. During the summer, Dad wanted Beau-the-brand-new-father out in the field with him at 6:30 in the morning, baling hay. After five months, Beau moved his little family out of the farmhouse and into an apartment in the village of Carmel. In February 1984, he moved his family back to Florida.

Paul was the foreman of the construction crew, but he

didn't have a supervisory bone in his body. He was a good old boy who, even as a child, had been happy to run toy tractors and cars and trucks in the sandpile all day long. Nowadays he drove a big four-wheel-drive Chevy truck and was happy to run bulldozers and earth-movers across acres of farmland all day long, turning it into subdivisions. He had never been one to tell others what to do; he had two bossy older sisters doing that. His strategy was the same one he used in the attempt to save his own life from Dad's fury at his inability to read: Lie low and disappear at the first opportunity.

Paul had squeaked through school with D's and F's, graduating third from the bottom of his class. Paul had Dad's mechanical skill as well as his learning disabilities; Dona, Beau, and I had our mother's intelligence, went to college, and either majored or minored in math.

Since Beau had an up-to-date familiarity with Dad's operations, he gave directions to Pat and Jeff, asked questions, and supplied tidbits of information. Dona brought a picture postcard that showed four donkeys (ahem) around a watering tank with the caption "Board of Directors."

We all agreed that Dad needed an estate plan, and when we brought Dad in at the end of the day to report to him what we had learned that day, he blew a gasket at our request for an estate plan. He wasn't planning to die. Fortunately, our last informant of the day was his lawyer and good friend, Willis Kunz. Being the same age as Dad, Willis breathed some reason into the moment.

That year, 1985, we met again in August, and we also did the intervention for our mother, who voluntarily went into a 28-day treatment program one week after she had moved into her new house, and three days after her divorce was final.

Where to go from here?

In 1986 Beau decided to move back to Indiana, yet again, to become Dad's general manager. Having tried it once, he knew the pitfalls. He asked that his and Paul's salaries be raised from $35,000 a year to $100,000 a year. Paul had certainly earned it.

The four of us met every year. For the first several years, Dona and I did special projects during our week in Indiana—writing up a personnel policy handbook or doing a systems analysis for a computer.

In 1988 I began financial consulting, going to Indiana for two weeks every three months and preparing budgets and cash-flow projects for Beau, the general manager.

Dad ran his companies by the seat of his pants, using his intuition. Beau was lost in the weekly and monthly loans made between companies, depending on where the cash was any particular moment, in order to meet the weekly payroll for 43 employees.

To analyze the situation, I broke Dad's catchall company, Fine Builders, into four "divisions"—land, construction, horses, and rental properties. Eventually, I figured out that if Wilfong Construction didn't break even in January and February, the muddy months, it would have a loss for the year. Paul and Dad were too tenderhearted and felt too responsible to lay off men when there wasn't enough work for them in the winter.

After ten years of family meetings, Beau found an

estate planner, so when Dad died in 1997, the year of our thirteenth annual meeting, the four of us were a well-oiled machine.

As the executor of Dad's estate, Beau typed up a three-page, single-spaced list of all the companies that the four of us held jointly in that first year, 1998. It had taken us thirteen years to prepare Dad's estate and to prepare ourselves for his death. Dad had roped us together financially with mutual, closely held investments that lasted another seventeen years.

Dad had repeatedly told us the story of Vera Hinshaw, who sued her four brothers and sisters after their parents died and thereby put a big dent in their inheritance. "Don't be like Vera Hinshaw!" Dad had warned us two or three times a year, especially when her name appeared in the local paper again and again as she sued the town, the planning board, the city council, or the rail trail.

Although he couldn't see it, these annual family meetings were the way we avoided the Vera pitfall. By all staying on the same page, and by being kind and extremely ethical with each other, we rode through the money minefield and arrived safely on the other side.

In 2002 Beau sold the water utility, and we faced the decision of whether to invest together or go our separate ways.

Beau was tired—tired of being the chief executive, tired of being his brother's and his sisters' keeper. Paul and I individually continued to invest with Beau, while Dona and her husband took their money into conservative investments that they felt more comfortable with.

The list of our common holdings shortened to two pages, then one page, then half a page.

In June 2014, on the occasion of our thirtieth family meeting, Beau announced the end of family meetings.

I am now as old as my dad was when we started these meetings. My own estate plan has been firmly in place for twenty years; Beau's for twenty-five years; Dona's for ten years. Paul, at age 62, is just now getting around to putting his plan in place due to the pressure from his lawyer, Katie Kunz, daughter of Dad's attorney, Willis Kunz.

We've had a very good run.

LIFE

THE PLAN

I THOUGHT MY LIFE WOULD go according to plan that winter day. I thought my life would follow the recipe card of my iPhone calendar. I thought I knew where I was going and when. I thought I was in control of my day.

But life rearranged itself. Perhaps it didn't like the way I had the reins cinched up too tight. Leaving home at eight in the morning and not returning till eight at night. So many places to go. So many things to do.

I did drive to meditation at 8:00 A.M. at my neighbors' house. I drove because I thought I would be driving on from there afterwards, driving to Putney, driving into my schedule.

But no. I had an extra twenty minutes, so I drove home and parked my car by the front door, in front of Bill's garage. And twenty minutes later, my nine-year-old Prius would not start. Oh, it had been cranky on the previous zero-degree days, but this January morning, despite the balmy nine degrees, my car would not start. Neither would it stop. It was caught in the limbo of a red power light and a green park light. Neither on nor off. Caught in the middle, as I now was. Despite the tumble of today's to-do, the car was unable to turn on.

Where is the Prius' battery, anyway? It has scads of batteries and they're hiding. I almost found the twelve-volt battery, in the corner of the hatchback, but it was enclosed, encased, inaccessible.

So Bill called AAA, and I threw my chores into the passenger seat of my pickup truck and left.

I didn't go to the bank. I didn't go to the post office. I did go to see my 82-year-old tenant and signed our lease, agreeing that she will stay another year and a half. At least that's the plan. But plans were not working out very well today.

I did go to my massage and was relaxing on the table under the hands of Kathryn, the masseuse, when someone knocked on the door. I've been going to this masseuse every week for fourteen years, and only twice has anyone knocked on the door. Bill, both times. Last October, he came armed with tweezers so he could remove a tick that Kathryn had found feasting on my upper arm. On this particular January day, Bill walked in, wearing a navy blue nylon parka and fogged glasses. "The tow truck came and jumped the car," he reported. "So I drove to the service station, and they're testing it there, across the street." And I am testing time and life and things to do.

He left. He returned as Kathryn massaged my head and face, easing anxiety from my countenance, which was counting on some things, but not these surprises that life was delivering. He said my car was running in the parking lot. Parked and running, both. "You need a new battery," he told me. "You have to go to the Toyota dealership."

My iPhone had run out of battery, too. Kathryn called for me, using her phone. Keene Toyota did have a battery in stock. I told them I'd be there at 12:30. They penciled me in for 1:00.

So at 1:00, I was sitting in the Toyota waiting room instead of in my writing group. And at 1:25, I heard my name called. "Cheryl. Your car is ready."

And I drove on into my expectations, into what was *supposed* to be happening, and I was overcome with gratitude at the grace of life that solves my so-called problems, without my assistance or control.

For there I was on a bright, cold, blue day in a warm blue car, driving to writing group, just as I had planned.

LOUISA VON TRAPP

My granddaughter, thirteen-year-old Chloe, is playing Louisa in *The Sound of Music* next month. Last week, the 99-year-old Louisa died. Actually, the third oldest von Trapp child was named Maria, not Louisa. Writers understand how confusing it is to have two characters with the same name. Therefore, for dramatic purposes, the thirteen-year-old Maria was renamed Louisa by the scriptwriters.

I sent Chloe the *New York Times* article about the death of the last von Trapp Family singer, and I wished her an equally long life. She was born in 2000, so that would bring her to 2099, just a few months shy of the new twenty-second century.

Can thirteen-year-olds look at a picture of an ancient, white-haired woman and think, "Wonder if I'll look like that"? Of course not. In their eyes, the old have always been old, their own parents have always been middle-aged, and they themselves—the young—are forever young.

They think life is fixed, even though almost every girl has seen photos of her mother as a little girl looking so similar to herself. My own mother was the same age as Shirley Temple, but no matter how many Shirley Temple movies I watched, I still had a hard time imagining my mother dancing and prancing as a little girl.

Even when I saw Shirley Temple Black as the United States representative to the United Nations, and even though I could see the little Shirley Temple in her, I couldn't conceive that I myself would be 33 or 55, and certainly not the hobbling 66 of my grandmother with her cane.

So, half a century later, this 66-year-old grandmother sends off an article to her thirteen-year-old granddaughter, who is delighted to be singing and dancing the part of Louisa von Trapp.

The 99-year-old Louisa/Maria has died. Although Chloe might imagine the world of the twenty-second century, she imagines herself as a thirteen-year-old in it. Well, maybe she has some indistinct children and a dog and a cat and a husband who looks vaguely like her dad.

But she can't imagine the deaths of those old people, now middle-aged people. One day, she herself will look back a century in time and look forward to the futures of her grandchildren a century hence. Beloved grandchildren, busy with their own lives, who believe they will be young forever.

WHAT IS FAMILY, ANYWAY?

When do you say good-bye to the family you loved as a child? You think the family is fixed, that it will always be there. At first, there are little cracks: cousins graduate from high school, one disabled cousin dies. The big kids get married and soon have babies.

Then your grandmother dies, and you realize that your dad is an orphan. But he still gets together with his brothers and sisters. You still go to family reunions, even though the in-laws get on each other's nerves.

Then you yourself graduate and go off to college and live a life that the people at home could never imagine. New friends, city living, biochemistry.

The time for saying good-bye has passed, and you didn't even notice. You still go home for the holidays and live there during the summer, but, really, you're not sure what your sister and brother are doing. Or your parents. You've never had to ask them before. You used to get this information by osmosis, and now there are big gaps, but you don't really notice that you don't know these people as well as you used to.

Later, decades later, you will make special efforts to say good-bye to friends or situations you know are leaving. Still, people slip away. You read an obituary and think, "Wait. I'm not ready to let them go. I didn't even know she was sick. And now she's gone. Gone. And I didn't say good-bye."

Your brother, your sister have children. You become an aunt or an uncle, active or distant. Then your own parents die, one after the other. You yourself become an orphan.

Meanwhile, your brother and sister become grandparents, and their attention is riveted to their grandchildren. Your cousins don't reunion anymore because their definition of family has changed. No longer does the clan of your relationship have much importance for them. Now, each one of them is the matriarch or the patriarch of their own tribe. They each reunion with the genetic copies of themselves.

My parents have died. My brothers live a thousand miles away, my sister three thousand miles. We have our own little reunion once a year. Just the four of us with a common set of DNA and memories. I remember what they were like when they were small. Now, they all have gray hair, or none.

Their children barely know each other as cousins; they don't find DNA that interesting, anyway.

For a few hours, my beloved family, sans our parents, will come together. Then we will disperse. Gone. Just like every other family the world has ever known. Gone. Really gone.

Adults who were children together are now somewhat jaded about each other's foibles, or worse, angry. Little bitternesses have added up to "Sorry, I won't be able to see you." The old definition of family—parents, grandparents, aunts, and uncles—no longer defines us. Now we are defined by our children, our grandchildren. The focus shifts to "my beloveds"—the cute children, the mirror images, sometimes, of ourselves.

The word "family" stays the same, and thereby disguises the ever-changing roster of members as well as our changing roles within this concept, this idea of family. "Family" (whatever that is) is a petri dish for what we call love—our attachment to these particular people. Who would we be without them?

As if such a thing as family actually exists.

THE OEDIPAL COMPLEX

I'M READING ANOTHER PHILOSOPHY book. Yes, my eyes glaze over after just a few sentences. But I find enough illuminated signposts to keep me slogging through the dense and muddy paragraphs that refer to Heidegger, Nietzsche, Freud, and Otto Rank. Who were those guys anyway? Yes, I've heard their names, but, other than Freud, I don't have a sense of what these philosophers represent.

Every several pages, the author refers to the Oedipal complex, or, as he has tweaked it, "the Oedipal project."

The Oedipal complex is wishing your parent to be dead. We've all had that thought, and we've all repressed it, hidden it underground in the psyche, to different depths. I never actually said to my parents, "I wish you were dead," but I remember sitting in my father's living room and idly inventorying what items I would like to get when he died. That's about as close as I came to allowing that repressed Oedipal wish some breathing space.

When my nephew was seven years old, he said to his mother (my sister), "I hate you."

And she calmly replied, "Sometimes I don't like you very much either."

There. That clears the air and says the unsayable.

My friend Carol's father-in-law died this year. "Nobody really liked him," she said. "No one will miss him." The man may have been conceited, but the repressed wish for one's own parent's death is sometimes only thinly veiled.

My friend, Maureen, in her early fifties, wished that her parents would give her some of her inheritance. She needed the money *now*. Instead, she had to twiddle her thumbs, waiting another ten years for her mother to die.

Adult children, who hold the key to the precious grandchildren, need more money. They are limping along on $35,000 a year, or maybe they are making ten times as much as their retired parents, yet they want more money for their children right now. They want their inheritance (i.e., wish their parent dead), so that they can give their precious children everything those children should have.

There's a Zen story about the villager who was so tired of his aging, complaining father that he wheelbarrowed the old man to the nearest cliff. His little boy wanted to go along with him. Just as the farmer was about to push his father over the cliff, complete with wheelbarrow, his little son said, "Wait. Save the wheelbarrow. I'll need it to carry you."

Several friends, in their sixties and even seventies, still have living parents. Jan's mother turned 100 in August. Oh, I am so thankful that I don't have decrepit, frail, and fragile parents still living. My mother died at 74, which seemed way too young, and my father died just shy of his eightieth birthday, which seemed a little too soon for me but just about right for his failing kidneys and the resulting spotty dementia that he abhorred.

After he died, I felt that a big oak tree had fallen in the forest and my own little tree suddenly had air to breathe and space to grow into. What a surprising relief to have the space to breathe, to flex my muscle, and to finally, finally be myself, shorn of shoulds I hadn't even known existed.

Just how do parents feel about those darling children whom they love so deeply and who certainly do love them so deeply in return . . . but still wish them dead?

Why else do teenage boys play violent video games? Just who are they repeatedly killing? The fathers whom they love so deeply and devotedly?

In olden days, royal families killed each other off. Shakespeare's tragedies are full of such betrayals. Sons (and daughters) want their rightful inheritance, whether or not they are royal.

As for that little mind game I played in my father's living room, after he died I didn't really want very much of his stuff anyway. It wasn't my style. I did take his comfortable kitchen chairs, which are on rollers.

I roll on through my life, now, reaching the age when nieces, nephews, or children might idly speculate how much they will inherit when I die.

COMMUNITY THANKSGIVING

The Community Thanksgiving Dinner in Brattleboro has been happening for 41 years—as long as I have lived here—and I've never gone, because I thought it was for losers. I didn't want to be a loser, so I thought if I didn't go, I wouldn't be one.

All this time, though, I've felt like a loser anyway. Living far away from family and not having children means I don't have those natural support networks. For whatever reason, or for no reason whatsoever, I'm not a person whom people invite over for fun. So I've often been lacking in invitations, and many times the people I've invited over have had something else to do.

I love to cook. And I love to cook a heavy carbohydrate meal like Thanksgiving dinner. I love to have leftovers. So often enough, it's just been Bill and me and a smallish turkey.

When Eva said she and Lawrence were going to the Community Thanksgiving Dinner because they were at loose ends, I said, "Okay, we'll meet you there." Melissa, who was within earshot, said she'd come too.

On Thanksgiving morning, Eva bailed out. So Bill and I met Melissa at two o'clock at the River Garden, where three dozen tables stood. The place was about half full. I knew half the people there. Even if I couldn't recall their names, I knew I had met them somewhere.

Because I volunteer at the Emergency Overflow Shelter once a week, I also recognized several of the street people about town who were there warming up or getting take-out meals for dinner. Actually, a few of those characters, whom I haven't seen this year sleeping on the floor of the Baptist church, were there and looking rather spiffed up.

Bill, Melissa, and I sat down beside Fred and Patrice and Fred's daughter Katherine, who has Down syndrome. We all talked for over an hour. Other friends and acquaintances came by, said hello, and gave us a hug. Some were volunteering for the huge effort it takes to serve 600 people a free meal. Others were just resting and digesting.

I had to ask myself, "What *was* I thinking?"

We love to go to community suppers for the potluck of not knowing who we're going to be sitting with. We go to the Dummerston Grange chicken-pie dinners, the Dummerston Church strawberry supper, the Dummerston Fire Department's pancake breakfast, the monthly Putney Community Dinners, even the Hunters' Breakfast in November. And every month Bill goes to his Sunday breakfasts at church.

All these years, and I have been the loser. Losing out on the community of Thanksgiving dinner.

PINE RIDGE

I FINALLY SAW THE MOVIE *Pow Wow Highway*, which was released in 1989. Jane, who spent two weeks every summer on the Pine Ridge Indian Reservation in South Dakota, home of the Oglala Lakota, had recommended it to me twenty years ago.

Oh, how I wanted to go live on the Pine Ridge Reservation back in August 1970—but alas, it was not to be. Our VISTA trainers assigned me to Utah, and I never again saw my fellow VISTAs who went to volunteer for a year on Pine Ridge.

I saw *Pow Wow Highway* as part of Bill's Rotary Club's Native American Film and Food Festival. They were raising money for radio station KILI on the Pine Ridge Reservation, which broadcasts in Lakota.

I took out a half-page ad in the program for my book *Following the Nez Perce Trail*, although I knew that I'd be lucky to sell two books. I designed the ad to include my best review: "The National Park Service should canonize this woman." Dr. Kent Nerburn wrote that review on the Amazon page for my guidebook. He himself wrote yet another book on Chief Joseph and had used my book as his Bible for the 1,170-mile pilgrimage.

Kent Nerburn has written several books, mostly

about the Lakota, and he's a good friend of John Willis, who lives on the other side of the mountain from me. John is a photographer who's been going to Pine Ridge for a month every July, ever since Jane recommended it to him twenty years ago.

The movie begins on the reservation of the Northern Cheyenne, in southeastern Montana. Filbert, who is obese, decides he's ready to become a warrior. He gets an iron pony—a 25-year-old Pontiac whose vinyl top is shredded.* He pays for it with a bag of hash, and his journey, his pilgrimage, begins with synchronicity.

His sort-of friend, Red Bow, wants to go to Santa Fe to get his sister out of jail, but while he's dozing in the passenger seat, Filbert heads to Bear Butte, South Dakota, even today a place of vision quests. Filbert leaves Red Bow sleeping in the car and walks up the butte to seek his warrior's vision. An ancient warrior comes to Filbert, who later finds a stone, which he puts into the medicine pouch hanging around his neck.

On May 8, 1987, I camped at Wolf Point, Montana, not so far from Bear Butte—west of the Lakota and east of the Assiniboine, north of the Cheyenne and south of the Cree. The next morning, as I sprinkled cornmeal to the four directions, thanking the spirits of that place for their protection, I saw a 200-year-old shaman, dressed in white buckskin and surprisingly short. He was an old man with long white hair. Then he was gone. And I continued

---

* Pontiac was an Ottawa war chief (1720–1769) responsible for Pontiac's War in 1763.

on my own quest, which was really just beginning. That year, I spent seven months on the road as one door after another opened, leading me into the book I would write, *Following the Nez Perce Trail*.

After Filbert's successful vision quest, *Pow Wow Highway* continues with problems and synchronistic solutions. Filbert's serene temperament and sacred vision provide the counterbalance to Red Bow's angry activism—two different styles of being a warrior.

The jailing of Red Bow's sister, it turns out, has been a setup to get Red Bow out of town—he asks too many good questions about the proposed strip mine on the reservation. The lawyers don't want him in the room when they sign the contracts.

In the end of the movie, Filbert's war pony breaks Red Bow's sister out of jail, and the two warrior-friends skedaddle back to the reservation in Lame Deer, Montana, in time to save the tribe from the developers.

Every movie is a depiction of a hero's or heroine's journey—the adventure from the known into the unknown. Perhaps one of the reasons *Pow Wow Highway* so appealed to me is that I was called to my own exploration in 1987 to research the Nez Perce Trail. I did a vision quest before embarking on that pilgrimage in April, and I did another vision quest in July, in the middle of my heroine's journey that year.

One of the many things my quest/pilgrimage did for me was to put me into a new relationship with my land-developer father. I broke out of the jail of doing what I thought he would approve of, and I followed my bliss instead. After those two years of research on the road, I could go back home, to Dad's office, and work for him on my own terms—two weeks every three months. He got what he so deeply desired, though not exactly in the form he wanted—his children to carry on his life's work. And through that, he got what he really wanted from me—love, acceptance, and forgiveness from one of those he most dearly loved.

EAST HILLSIDE

I FOUND A GARDEN STATUE at Allen Brothers farm stand in June and bought it without consulting Bill. The price was right—$32. Bill cuts down enough trees—leaving several stumps scattered through the woods—that we have lots of display stands ready and waiting for another statue.

This one, called Sitting Indian, is a modernist sculpture of a long-haired Native American woman sitting, knees curled to one side—the way that women sit in the temples in Thailand. Unusually, this concrete statue is stained in various shades of reddish rust, making her whole appearance unique and inviting.

Where to put her? Bill chose a stump we can see out the backdoor window on what I call the east hillside. At the far end of that little hillside, about a hundred feet away, sits a statue of another Native American woman, her eyes downcast.

When I first built my house, in 1980, I woke up every day and looked out my bedroom's east window to the trees on the east hillside. I repeatedly felt certain that a Native American woman was buried on that hillside, but, of course, how could I ever know that as a fact?

Sometimes I meandered through the trees, but found no sign of anything other than forest.

A few years later, I was led on a quest to write a guidebook to the Nez Perce Trail. After the idea had hatched, but before I had any idea I was actually going to do the project, a past-life reader told me I had been a Nez Perce woman in my most recent past life. In that incarnation, I had tried to bring peace between the races, but that lifetime had been a poor leverage point in which to do that.

Unexpectedly, I did follow my bliss: I followed that 1,200-mile trail and put 35,000 miles on my truck while doing the research. This pilgrimage took me to every historical spot along the route. I returned home and wrote the manuscript. A publisher miraculously appeared, and my book was published.

Only years later did I realize that the woman on the east hillside no longer called to me. Now her grave is marked by two garden statues of Native American women—unknown and unnamed and forgotten by all, except those who feel her in their bones.

HEAT PUMP

My house is 32 years old, and it's getting one more piece of new furniture. I went down to the basement to see the delivery. Actually it's two pieces. The unexpected piece looks like a smallish water heater, white and round with two round openings where pipes attach.

The second and the main attraction is the heat pump, about twice the size of our propane furnace, a sort of squished version of our small chest freezer. The various pipes on the wall make our basement look like a ship's engine room—there are four zones for the propane furnace, and now two zones for the geothermal heat pump.

Our plan is to heat two rooms by using water from our well. So a new water line has been installed beside the old one that runs from the well to the house. The six-foot-deep trench was fascinating to behold, but terrifying to anticipate, since it ran through two flower beds and the strip of lawn that separates them. The shrubs I had planted around the well head to camouflage it were pretty well demolished within a three-foot radius of the well. And by the time the very small Kamamoto excavator backed into place, a redbud, a pine, and a rhododendron were knocked down. My variegated Fontansia shrub, which was six feet away, surprisingly disappeared.

Sigh. The price of progress is that I have raw new flowerbeds, not quite in the same location as the old ones.

The trench was fascinating because the excavator hit ledge six feet down, and water immediately seeped into the trench. "Oh, the water's running on top of the ledge," said Guy from Green Mountain Well. "No doubt about that," he concluded as he repacked his cheek with snuff.

The cellar wall now has a new hole in it for the water line that will return water from the closed system to the well.

Here's the scheme: the well water comes in at 55 degrees, runs through the heat pump, which extracts ten degrees of the heat in it, then returns to the well at 45 degrees. It seems like a mystery that 55 degrees is going to heat a room, but think of your refrigerator. You could say that heat is extracted from inside the box and that the back side of the box generates heat. This heat is stored in the new little water tank that will then run into three radiators. *Voilà!* Heat.

The electricity it takes to run the well pump, the heat pump, and the water tank comes from the 59 solar-voltaics on the roof.

Of course, I feel anxious about being an early adopter of this newish technology. It's actually hard to be the first on my block; it requires a leap of faith (or several). How much electricity will it use? How much noise will it make? How much heat will it produce? And how in the world are we going to rearrange our basement? That clutter down there will have to find a new home.

So this is the real price of progress: doubt and apprehension. Doubt prevents forward movement. Apprehension keeps the mind busy with "yes, buts." I try to calm my qualms by reminding myself that we are not using fossil fuel. We are substituting the sun for coal-fired electricity, and water for propane. Sun and water are renewable; we can sustain this system forever, without needing to go to war over oil.

Peace descends upon my mind.

MILK OF HUMAN KINDNESS

When November cold arrives, the Emergency Overflow Shelter opens its doors to the parlor of the Baptist Church. It begins with dinner at 5:30 every evening, prepared and served by volunteers from one local church or another. Then the first pair of volunteers arrives for the 7:00 P.M. to 1:00 A.M. shift. This is my fourth year volunteering, and my third year of signing up for the stepchild second shift of 1:00 A.M. to 7:00 A.M. Volunteers are a bit scarce, so I'm always sitting by myself at the volunteer table, which is lit by one lamp that looks as if it came from a thrift store.

I take with me a big, long, boring project that I would never spend time doing during daylight hours. On my first week, I typed up three months worth of essays from my writing workshop. The next week, I took in a two-year-old pile of photos and newspaper clippings and simply sorted them by year. The following week, I put them into photo albums.

Beginning at five, I make fresh coffee and refill the urn as needed for the early risers. These street people do get an early start to their day.

I keep working on my project-of-the-week until wake-up call at six. Then I put everything away and knit for the final hour, keeping a more alert eye on the men who are yawning, stretching, and farting as they wait in line for the one very small bathroom.

A young man named Ryan came in at 5:30 one morning.

"You're supposed to check in by ten," I said in my mildest voice.

"The police found me in an elevator and told me to come here," he said in a pathetic voice as he began to shiver visibly. "I'm so cold. The elevator was warm."

I went to the closet and found a clean sleeping bag and a clean pillow. As I handed them to him, I said, "Wake-up call is at six."

At 6:30, Lucie, the director of the Brattleboro Area Drop-In Center as well as this shelter, came in. She's a past-middle-age busy woman, constantly cleaning or straightening whatever is within arm's reach.

While I remained seated at the volunteers' table, she walked over to the parlor side of the room, which has three sofas, a couple of easy chairs, and the VCR, which is turned off at 10:00 P.M.

"Wake up," I heard her say. "You have to be out of here in half an hour."

Ryan stumbled around, and now he sounded drunk. "I'm never coming back here," he said.

"Here's tape and a Sharpie," I told him, "so you can put your sleeping bag into a black trash bag and mark it with your name. That way you'll have it the next time you come."

He didn't take the tape or the Sharpie, and he left his plastic bag on the floor ten feet away from his sleeping bag, which was now on the path to the bathroom.

"You think I'm a loser," he told me, "but I'm not." And with that he stormed out the door.

"I guess you should wash these," I said to Lucie and handed her the abandoned sleeping bag and pillow.

I left a few minutes later. Fortunately, I had written myself a note, which was sitting on the passenger seat waiting for me: milk.

Eight minutes north of the Baptist church, I turned right onto Carpenter Road. A 1980 Mercedes behind me also turned.

Wow, I thought. *He must be picking up milk at Jillson's, too.*

I stopped in front of the tiny shed where Bonnie distributes the milk every evening and every morning into half-gallon Mason jars, then puts them into the refrigerator with a quart of two of cream from her five Jersey cows. Usually eight or ten dozen eggs are sitting on the bottom shelf as well.

So this Mercedes is picking up his milk too?

The driver motioned to me through our car windows. When I got out, he got out. "You have a flat tire," he said.

I looked at the rear tire on the driver's side. It was about two inches away from flat-out flat. "Oooh," I sighed, already thinking of AAA, phone calls, waiting, drumming my fingers. I just wanted to go home and take a nap in bed with Bill.

"I've got a tire inflator," he said. "It plugs into your cigarette lighter."

"Okay," I said as I took the cord, plugged it in, and turned on my Prius. I uncapped the tire, and he fitted on the inflating hose. Three minutes later, I had a tire big enough to drive on.

"Are you on your way somewhere?" I asked. I was wondering how he had enough time to make this eight-minute side trip.

"Oh, I work the night shift at the Retreat, on the addictions unit, and I'm just on my way home," said this Good Samaritan of an early and chilly November morning.

FACEBOOK PHOTOS OF OUR NEAREST AND DEAREST

A NEIGHBOR SAYS SHE'S UNFRIENDING people on Facebook who post recipes. I understand her point of view. I'm thinking of unfriending people who post pictures of themselves with a giant, sloshing goblet of sangria, or their lunch at the brew-pub with a pregnant friend, or even just the label from a bottle of wine.

Mostly, on Facebook, people post photos of their nearest and dearest—those sweet children or grandchildren. I have to remember that the ones who post photos of wine bottles or growlers of beer are also posting photos of their nearest and dearest. They couldn't live without these dear spirit-friends. Those bottles are the most important relationships in their lives, despite the lip service they give to the "darling husband" or the "wonderful wife" or the "I-love-them-to-pieces children." They spend more time every day planning their rendezvous with their bottle than they spend thinking about picking up the kids after school. These bottles are their secret affairs of the heart, the real love of their life. They even carry little bottles of booze with them, in their pocket or their pocketbook, so they'll never be separated from the one they love the most.

A picture is worth a thousand words, and the pictures on Facebook speak volumes.

NOT FACEBOOKING

A MIRACLE HAS HAPPENED. I haven't looked at Facebook in six months. Oh, I did complain for a few years that Facebook was a time sink, but I wasn't able to pry myself away from it.

To begin with, in 2009 I tried to friend a lot of people, even people I had met only once, as a way to promote my book. So now, I have 1,368 friends, and I do not see the vast majority of their posts. FB decides for me whose posts I see, and it's a rather limited number.

Meanwhile, though I post to my *Meditative Gardener* FB page every day, and although 996 people "like" *The Meditative Gardener*, only 23 people actually see the TMG posts. "Boost your posts," FB begs me. "Get 1,000 people to Like your page." Why would I pay a few dollars for a few seconds of people's attention before sinking back to "23 people viewed this post"?

Once or twice a week, people I see around town tell me they've seen one of my *Meditative Gardener* posts, so I know, contrary to my FB numbers, that people *do* see what I write.

So why am I on Facebook? To promote my book—just to keep it in the back of people's minds. And my personal page? Mostly I use it to brag. "Went to aerial yoga this morning and hung upside down for ten minutes." Or "Bill and I hiked Mt. Okemo. That's 1,900 feet up and 1,900 feet down. Oh, my aching knees."

I've given up on my TMG Facebook page as a promotional tool, though I continue to post to it daily. My blog offers me a direct link to posting on FB, so I don't actually go to the Facebook page.

Each one of the social networking sites listed below wants to capture my attention and keep me on their website. They do not want me to turn my attention loose on something as magnetic as Facebook and be lost to them for the rest of the day. FB sends me three or four e-mails a week, as if they're my best friend, even though I opted out of notifications years ago.

During the winter months, I would sometimes spend half an hour or more scrolling though my personal FB page, "liking" various people's posts. What was I doing? Clicking the mouse, pressing the bar like a rat in a cage, hoping for something positive. I began clicking "Like," whether I liked it or not, just so I would continue to see posts from those particular people.

Pressing "Like" says, *Yoo-hoo. I'm here. I see you. Yes, you're a real person. And I'm your friend, though I don't have time to actually talk to you. But I do think about you. For these two seconds. For these two seconds, I care about you.*

For a long time, I thought Facebook was a good way to keep up with people. What are my nieces and nephews doing? And that meditation friend? Or the high school friend I haven't seen in years? Really, I mean, *really*, what's the purpose of that? Information in, information out. Gone.

In March, I came back from three weeks of retreats—retreating from books, retreating from writing, and retreating from the enticement of cyberspace. I went back to e-mail, but I haven't been back to Facebook. It's a miracle.

> Facebook—Who I am.
>
> LinkedIn—Who I am professionally.
>
> Twitter—Who I am right this minute.
>
> Pinterest—Who I want to be.
>
> Google Plus—What I think.
>
> Instagram—How I want to be perceived and received by the world. (Romancing my life.)

VALUATION

If I were a valuable person, I would have valuable things. But I still live in my house, which I built in 1979 for $55,000, and which I added on to in 1988 for $100,000.

If I were a person of taste, I would drink fine wines and be able to discuss the subtleties of flavors and brands. But mostly I drink water from my 120-foot well, and it has no taste at all.

If I were a rich person, I would eat rich foods at fine restaurants and not blink at the multihundred-dollar check as I handed over my American Express card. But I like to eat at local restaurants, some of which accept personal checks but not credit cards.

If I were a person of the upper crust, then I wouldn't eat crusts at all. But I love crusty breads from local bakers, especially Beni's Swiss whole-wheat walnut bread.

If I were flush I would sit on a high throne and my feet wouldn't touch the ground. But my toilets are water-savers, and we flush only when it's brown.

If I were a stylish person, I would buy expensive clothes of the latest style or redecorate my home. But I buy my clothes at a thrift store, which only goes to show that I am thrifty. Does secondhand mean second-class?

If I were really classy, then I would hobnob with people of the upper class. I would stay at five-star hotels. But every summer my favorite vacation is a week of camping with my neighbors.

If I were a jewel of a person, then I would wear jewels and gems, but I've given up wearing the modern version of shackles—bracelets and necklaces—and only wear earrings hand-made by local artisans.

If I were a precious person, I would wear precious stones. But in April I take off the rings that Bill gave me and don't put them on until gardening season ends in November. Since I live in New England, I'm constantly throwing stones *out* of the garden.

If I were a treasure of a person, I would have a treasure chest of beautiful sparkly, shiny, golden things. Instead, people trust me to be the treasurer of their organizations (three at the present time).

If I were a person of stature, then I would be taller than I am, or maybe I would wear platform shoes. Instead I seem to be shrinking, and my aging feet require no-heel shoes with orthotics.

If I were a person of worth, then I would have a high net worth. But I do worthwhile things, like volunteer for hospice and for the homeless shelter.

If I were a person of substance, then I would have substantial things. The most substantial things I own, by size, are a 2,000-square-foot house, a pickup truck, a car, and a computer.

If I were a secure person, then I would invest in securities, and I would have a security system for my house. But I don't lock my house at night, and I leave my keys in my car. That's how secure I am.

If I were a trustworthy person, then perhaps I would have a trust fund. Instead I trust my funds to my local bank, Brattleboro Savings & Loan.

What makes a person truly valuable? High net worth, securities, a treasure chest of jewelry? Do outer trappings measure a person's worth? The wealthy remain unsatisfied; they want more and more, hoping that "more" will lead to happiness, thinking that "more" will lead to their escape from the inner feeling of unworthiness that we all, in this society, have.

A worthy person is ethical, generous, kind, friendly, and compassionate. These are qualities that cannot be found in the garnering of more and more.

Only after deep reflection do we begin to see that "more" means more stress—with maintaining and protecting what we have. "More" means more dissatisfaction as we continue to compare ourselves to others who have more than we do. We are trying to fill up an internal sense of lack that can never be filled with more material goods.

Do we want to spend our energy on the accumulation of material goods or on the practice of goodness? When we come to the end of our lives, we have to leave our material goods behind. Often enough, our treasures, and even our beautiful houses, become mere junk that our children don't really want.

The skill of goodness includes being contented, being satisfied with what we already have. When we have an inner sense of sufficiency, our outer circumstances, whatever they are, will also feel sufficient.

Our goodness ripples out in ways we cannot imagine. Our good deeds are the real legacy we leave, not only to our children and family, but to our entire community.

FOUR CLASSES AT THE CIRCUS SCHOOL

I DID SOMETHING RADICAL THIS year—I signed up for four courses at the circus school. I've been taking trapeze for three years. Right now, I'm taking Trapeze 101 for the thirteenth time. Chloe, who was in my second trapeze class, has now completed the Professional Training track at the New England Center for Circus Arts. This fall, she's teaching Stretching 101.

My fellow student, age 24, is my teacher. I'm old enough to be her grandmother. She doesn't let her grandmother see her five tattoos, though, because her grandmother would be upset. I've seen them all.

Chloe was a powerhouse in Trapeze 101. What she lacked in grace, she made up for in muscle. She simply powered her way into positions on the trapeze, positions that I still struggle with.

My friend Paul was Chloe's softball coach when she was in fifth grade in Langdon, New Hampshire. She was so strong, even then, that he was afraid she'd run right over the littler girls on her team. Maybe that explains her team spirit. She not only looked out for the peanut-sized girls when she was young, she looked out for me when we were in trapeze class together.

One of the reasons I took trapeze in the first place was to grapple with a deep-seated sense of being on the outside, feeling left out. When I was in sixth grade, during recess, Beth Hanna, Sandy Molden, and Marilyn Fatzinger started whispering to each other. "You're too little, Cheryl," they said. "Go away."

I went and played on the monkey bars by myself while they shared their secrets. In retrospect, they were probably whispering about their periods. Beth was five-foot-six and wore a straight skirt, hose, and flats. I was four-foot-ten, 55 pounds, with anklets and saddle oxfords. I was definitely the peanut in that crowd.

In doing The Work weekly, a method of questioning my stressful thoughts, I often came back to this scene, and I was good and tired of it. *Okay, then,* I told myself. *Go play on the monkey bars, even though you're 63 years old, and just see how it feels.*

Trapeze class was as close as I could get to monkey bars, and I knew that I was opening myself up to weekly attacks of feeling like an outsider among five or ten twenty-somethings who had been gymnasts or dancers or athletes their entire lives. I didn't exercise when I was a peanut because I'd been severely asthmatic as a child, and exertion often induced wheezing.

But I survived my first trapeze class and then my second trapeze class with Chloe. That particular class of twelve had so much esprit de corps that we performed a recital at the Cotton Mill Hill artists' holiday sale the first weekend of December 2011.

My group of three, including Mansell, who was 54, performed our routine to a very slow, peaceful melody, which gave me plenty of time to get from one position to another. Then Chloe and her two teenage teammates performed the same routine to a rocking, body-beating song as they simply swung themselves up onto the bar.

For me, that class with Chloe was the beginning of feeling at home at the circus school, so I also signed up for Circus Fit—a cross-training sort of exercise class starting with half an hour of stretching, moving to half an hour of aerobic cardio exercise, and concluding with half an hour of using the trapeze as a workout prop for pull-ups and shoulder shrugs.

After two years of this schedule, I added in Stretching 101, which took place just before trapeze class. On Thursday evenings, then, I had a three-hour workout. I've never before in my life worked out for three hours in a row, and, afterward, I was tired. I was pooped.

When my favorite aerial teacher, Ukoiya, offered a class on aerial yoga on Wednesday mornings, I couldn't resist. So I signed up for my fourth class at the circus school. Aerial yoga uses a fabric hammock as a prop to add stretchiness to the usual yoga asanas. Sometimes we lie on our stomachs in our fabric hammocks and become Balinese flying mermaids. Sometimes we hang upside-down in butterfly position for five minutes. Oh, does that feel good!

It's radical: four classes every week at the circus school for a 66-year-old woman who doesn't like to exercise.

But the results are good. I am a bit more flexible: I can sit in meditation for 45 minutes again without my hip getting cranky, something I haven't been able to do for the last fifteen years. In fact, at a recent retreat, I actually sat on a cushion, meditating, for two hours.

I am a bit stronger: I have biceps for the first time in my life. My left triceps is still an old-lady wing, flapping loosely on the underside of my arm, but my right triceps is almost snug. I have more endurance for gardening, hour after hour. I still can't rock 'n' roll to sit on the trapeze, nor can I hold the ropes and lift myself off the trapeze bar, so I haven't graduated into Trapeze 102.

Meanwhile, on Facebook I've watched Chloe perfect her splits. Recently, my yoga-teacher friend Josephine, who's seven weeks younger than I am, said she can do the splits on a good day. The gauntlet has been thrown down. In Circus Fit, we sometimes work on our splits for half an hour.

What I lack in power, I make up for with stick-to-itiveness. And whenever I think back on that monkey bars scene, I now imagine myself doing all sorts of monkey business.

STRETCHING

Sometimes, when I'm reading in bed, I catch a glimpse of my arm that's holding the book. I'm always startled to see the skin of my upper and lower arm looking like crepe paper, looking like the skin of a 75-year-old woman. I have a morbid fascination with the skin of my right arm and keep looking at it like something at a freak show, a physical oddity I can gaze at without interruption.

In stretching class at the circus school, I'm always the oldest. The forty-somethings can just about keep up with the instructor and over time make actual progress toward their splits. The 22-year-old is working toward being a contortion artist. She lies belly-down on the floor and touches her toes to her head. She's working on lying on her chest and touching her feet to the floor in front of her so that she looks like a mating dragonfly.

Meanwhile, I sit on the floor and do a side stretch. While relaxing my left arm beside my straddled left leg, I bend my right arm overhead to reach toward my left toes. I gaze upwards, directly into the crook of my right arm and am shocked to see the flaccid flesh of an 85-year-old. That's *my* arm?

The elasticity of my skin is going, going, gone—like the elastic waistband of my twenty-year-old pants that sag down toward my hips when I put the weight of my iPhone in my pocket. I keep hopefully hitching up my pants, but really, either they need new elastic or I need to give them back to the thrift store.

When I was twenty or forty, I thought my smooth skin *was* me. Why did old women let themselves go like that? I wasn't going to let that happen to me. Ha! As if "I" could stop it.

Gravity. Gravity wins over willpower as my underarm "wings" flap loosely, even as I'm showing off the best biceps I've ever had in my life. Gravity pulls me earthward, so I'm an inch and a quarter shorter than I used to be. A friend tells me that losing two inches of height is a sign of osteoporosis, but so far, my circus workout in the air is keeping my bone density well above the score for osteopenia, the precursor to osteoporosis.

So here's the conundrum: I don't want my skin to stretch, but I do want to stretch my muscles and ligaments. The skin stretches of its own accord, but I really have to work to stretch my straddles and my shoulders, my hip flexors and my hamstrings.

So I take my body to the trapeze bar, and, pretending that I'm ten years old, I swing my foot up to the bar and pull myself up so that I'm hanging from my knees. Stretching my torso upside down, I reverse the effects of gravity for a few seconds as I start to swing back and forth to gather momentum to reach for the ropes.

Did I think that stretching class wouldn't eventually stretch my body's elastic into a looser fit? The body bag of skin I live in is stretching out of shape and wrinkling and sagging like an old balloon. My muscles and skeleton are stronger, though, and I'm in better shape than I was a few years ago.

Really, there's no reason for me to get bent *out* of shape about my saggy skin. People come in all shapes and sizes, even in a single lifetime.

THINNING HAIR

WHEN MY DAD WAS 45, he ran for the Indiana state legislature on the single issue of pari-mutuel betting. He had his photo taken at the local photographer's, and Mother went to pick up the proofs. Before Dad arrived home that evening, Mother's artistic hand had penciled in some hair on the photo of Dad's balding pate.

Twenty-five years later, my brothers complained about losing their hair, and I snickered. Twenty-five years after that, my nephews complained about losing their hair, and I smiled and nodded.

What I didn't realize is that I, a 66-year-old woman, would also start losing the hair on *my* head.

Oh, I was happy to notice the hair disappearing on my legs, so that now just a few thin, pale brown hairs remain on the insides of my calves. The hair under my arms has become a wisp, though I wistfully recall the erotic sensations of that luxurious underarm hair. Finally, I feel no qualms about wearing sleeveless shirts. No fear that young men will spit out their disgust: "What are you—French?"

I sigh at the thinning of my pubic hair, and all the other activity that has thinned down there as well. When my mother was dying at age 74, I was shocked the first time I changed her diaper to see that no pubic hair at all remained. At age twelve, I had been so embarrassed at the swimming pool to see my mother's pubic hair extending down the insides of her thighs—"M*other!*" Forty years later, nothing. No hair at all.

Leg hair, underarm hair, pubic hair, all thinning. Still, I didn't see it coming. The hair on my head! Thinning. My definition of womanliness thinning out as well.

The men at my family reunion are a bunch of shiny billiard balls sitting in lawn chairs and telling stories under the shade of a big oak tree. In his seventies, my dad asked my brother to look at a bump on his "forehead", and pointed to a spot on the top of his head.

To disguise my thinning hair, I've adopted bangs to fluff up my scalp and act as camouflage. I call this move my comb-over, although it's more like a comb-forward. Bangs actually make me look younger.

Bill had a comb-over when I met him, when he was 52. He despaired at the loss of his full head of hair. I kept taking photos of his comb-over drooping down over his right ear. Finally, five years later, he allowed twelve-year-old Suzannah to cut it off. I keep telling Bill I love his bald head. While he's sitting in a chair, I sometimes massage his scalp playfully when I walk past him. He does not like my comb-forward (my bangs), but other people think I look cute.

My grandmothers continued in their old age to wear the hairstyles of their past. Mom Wilfong wore those 1930s finger waves right into the bouffant era of the early 1960s, when she died. Now I'm retro, too, wearing Mamie Eisenhower bangs like those I wore sixty years ago. Except now, those bangs are quite functional: they provide enough fluff to disguise the thinness of my hair.

Instead of telling Bill to shave off all the sparse hair on his head, maybe I should shave my head, like my brother Beau does, and join the crowd sitting under the spreading family tree.

WRECKAGE

My neighbor Connie's car has a dent in the door to the back seat. She was in town, while having dinner with a friend, when a teenager backed out of her driveway and into Connie's car, parked across the street. The dents to our physical vehicles come when we're not looking: a wrinkle here and there, a strain, a sprain, an ache, a pain.

Age is wrecking my body as well as everyone else's over the age of fifty. At first, you don't realize that things are loosening up. Or tightening up to the point where something needs lubricating.

By sixty, you begin to have a vague feeling that your body is skating on thin ice. Then, by seventy, you see people falling around you in the silent battle called Life. Some are successfully triaged. The local hospital ships them and their heart to the university hospital where medical miracles happen, and four days later, they walk out of the hospital, still unaware that they were about to be dead.

My friend Trudy told me that her 88-year-old heart is now fibrillating. When I met her twelve years ago on a trip to Turkey, she said that if she still lived in Turkey, as she did from age twelve to twenty-two, she'd be dead.

She was taking a heart medication called Coumadin that enables her to live her very full life with grace.

In her eighties, those activities have slowly peeled away. A double knee surgery at 82 spelled the end of doubles tennis. She still swims and paints every day, though, and volunteers at two nursing homes, the well-baby program, and a soup kitchen.

On her 87th birthday, she took her paints to her favorite place, which involved clambering down a rocky bank to the river. She fell on the rocks and rescued herself, then went to see her doctor about bruises and contusions, but fortunately, there were no fractures. The following winter, she took herself to the hospital for pneumonia.

The aging process wrecks all of us, each in her own way. A dear, sweet flower-gardening friend, age seventy, has brain cancer.

Aging always wins this game of Life, no matter how much we complain about her. We may not like how aging dents and wrecks the body of our vehicle, but she's trying to show us a simple truth. A truth we don't really want to see or hear or contemplate.

TIBETAN PRAYER WHEEL

For my December birthday, Whit and Tonia gave me a solar-powered Tibetan prayer wheel in gold plastic. The sort of kitsch you see on Asian dashboards, the sort of kitsch Asian friends give you as a hostess present. So full of merit and what-the-heck-am-I-supposed-to-do-with-this?

I've been to a number of Yankee Swaps with Whit and Tonia—the kind of post-Christmas, white-elephant gift-giving where you get to pass on the Christmas present that made you roll your eyes. When it's your turn, you can choose a gift someone else has already opened at the party or a freshly re-wrapped present. Usually there's a hot grab on two or three of the gifts. The rest you couldn't give away—literally. One year, it was Mary-in-a-bathtub (a plastic statue of the Blessed Virgin in a grotto); another year, a Viking helmet with horns and long blond braids for your inner Brünnhilde; one year, it was Bob the Singing Bass.

When I opened the box with the prayer wheel and raised my eyebrows to Whit, he said, "We've got one, too. Our friend in Nepal sent us two, and it seemed like the perfect gift for you."

So I decided to bite the gold plastic bullet, and I set the little solar-powered Tibetan prayer wheel on the window sill, and there it spun from the time the sun hit it at breakfast until early winter sunset at 4:30. The prayer wheel looks like a bell. Inside the bell is a prayer written on a piece of paper. For every rotation, a prayer is sent to heaven. I counted myself fortunate to have it.

One month later, Tonia was playing her usual Friday morning round of doubles tennis, but she couldn't lift the racket. "I feel weak today," she said, so she drove home.

Whit happened to be home and recognized her symptom as a woman's heart attack. He had had a cardiac arrest nine months previously and had learned the symptoms of heart attack in cardio rehab. He decided not to call an ambulance, but put Tonia in his car and drove to the hospital. The pain struck while they were on the interstate, eight minutes away from Brattleboro Memorial Hospital.

As soon as Tonia arrived at the hospital, the medicos doped her with morphine for the pain and put her in an ambulance bound for Dartmouth-Hitchcock Hospital an hour away in Lebanon, New Hampshire. There they put in a stent and gave her an anticoagulant. Then she had another heart attack and another stent and more anticoagulant and a rat's nest of tubes running into and out of her.

She came home after four days, and two weeks later she flew to England to be with her daughter for the birth of Tonia and Whit's new grandson.

Thanks to the experts at Dartmouth-Hitchcock and to those zillions of prayers from the solar-powered Tibetan prayer wheels, the circle of life keeps spinning around for Tonia and her new grandbaby.

LOU'S MEMORIAL SERVICE

At Lou's memorial service in February, I signed the register and started to watch the slide show of her life. Tears immediately came to my eyes; I didn't have a Kleenex and no one else was crying. Maybe 4:00 was too early to cry. Maybe I should wait until five, when the actual memorial service was to begin.

I walked into the room where rows of chairs had been set up in the community center, found a box of tissues, and sat down amid the quiet chitchat of people talking about their lives to each other. Why I felt so deeply bereft, I couldn't figure out. I didn't really know Lou that well, yet here I was, crying as if she were a member of my family.

I had barely dampened my Kleenex before the man sitting next to me distracted me into conversation. After fifteen minutes, I had totally stopped thinking about Lou, so I excused myself to look at the hundreds of cards she had received after her diagnosis of brain cancer in October. The dozens and dozens of cards were strung like garlands across two walls of old-time blackboards.

Bill and I had sent five cards, sort of in a hurry, because I had only learned of her illness in early February, and she died on February 19. During my last look at

CaringBridge.org, Lou's page had had more than 1,600 visits.

What was it about Lou that affected me so strongly? I knew her socially, and she had attended one of the classes I taught on Buddha's Brain. She, an RN, had actually taught me something about neuroscience in that class.

I was wishing I had known Lou better. Her obituary told the story of a remarkable woman–a Peace Corps volunteer in Afghanistan in 1964, a Peace Corps trainer for nurses going to Afghanistan in 1967 with the mission to wipe out smallpox in the only country in the world where it was still endemic.

She married Tom, who worked for CARE, and over the course of his thirty-year career they lived in India (where their children were born), the Philippines, Tunisia, the Congo, Egypt, and Washington, D.C. Lou was so outgoing that it was easy to imagine her as the wife who kept the home front together. But she had also had important nursing jobs wherever she went—Peace Corps Medical Officer in Tunisia and U.S. Embassy Medical Officer in the Congo and in Egypt.

When they retired to their home on the West River in 2002, they became loyal volunteers for many local services—organizations that I myself love.

Soon, I returned to socializing and hearing more stories of each person's relationship to Lou. For Lou always connected with people, always relating, relating, relating, from her cheerleading days at Greenville High School (Class of 1960), through her RN training, and on and on.

I did not cry during the memorial service as family and

friends spoke of their relationships to this sweet North Carolina native with the beguiling southern accent. Lou was someone who never met a stranger. One memorial rang especially true: "Where Lou was was home."

Yes, Lou felt like home. She came right up and talked to me at Perennial Swappers meetings as if we were old friends, or maybe family. Mostly we gardeners don't know each other's names, just our faces, but within a couple of biweekly meetings, everyone knew Lou.

I was figuring out that Lou did indeed feel like family—my family. She felt like my cousin Nancy, an outgoing cheerleader in her class of 1960, who died of cancer twenty years ago. My grief for Lou was all mixed up with my old grief for Nancy, whom I also did not know well enough.

The thing Lou taught me in the Buddha's Brain class is that when our old reptilian brain goes into fight-flight-or-freeze mode, all the energy goes to the big muscle groups. For a few seconds, our other bodily systems are put on the back burner—the cardiovascular system, the endocrine system, the digestive system, the respiratory system. For a few seconds, these systems are undernourished. Every time we worry or complain, every time we feel anxious, frustrated, or irritated, every time we have a thought, our bodies contract and are ready, ever so slightly, to fight the situation, flee from it, or just freeze into not-knowing. Multiply a few seconds of anxiety or worry or irritation by several times an hour. After days, years, and decades of the body tensing itself and being undernourished, a chronic disease develops.

Lou came to meditation in order to cope with her high blood pressure. She attended a few Sunday morning sits, but then her constant stream of visitors got the upper hand. Everyone loved to be around Lou, and friends came from near and far. She suffered the stress of preparing for their visits and the eustress of catching up with old friends, and making sure they felt at home.

She had a year of vertigo, which interfered something terrible with her gardening because she couldn't bend over. And then, just after she turned seventy, she couldn't do crosswords anymore.

When she received the diagnosis of brain cancer, her husband, always the dry wit, said, "No, that's not the way it's supposed to be. You're supposed to take care of me. You're the nurse."

But Lou had received confirmation of her one-way ticket, and her many friends and family could only go with her so far.

She lost her words except for "I love you" and "I'm fine." And those words she said to everyone she saw, until her son and daughter came for their last visit. And then she was gone.

BEST OF THE BLOG 2014

THE HEAVENLY MESSENGERS

AGING, ILLNESS, AND DEATH

www.themeditativegardener.blogspot.com

DYED DAISIES

For Valentine's Day, Bill bought me a bouquet of daisies at the supermarket. Daisies in my favorite pink and magenta colors. Dyed daisies.

"Dyed daisies?" he asked. "How do you know they're dyed?"

Well, first of all, their leaves are maroon. And secondly, the water in the vase is now pink from the color slowly leaching out of the stems.

He felt cheated. I still love looking at this ever-so-vibrant bouquet.

We expect our flowers to be natural, to have the *au naturel* look, so naturally (ahem) my sweetie feels cheated when he finds out the flowers have been "made up" to look more beautiful. I'm very fortunate that he likes my *au naturel* looks, because my beauty leached away some years ago.

Good looks leach away from all of us. When we're young, we're cute or maybe even beautiful. Some people's good looks stick longer than others. But one thing for sure: we will all wind up just like the daisies. Beautiful today. Faded tomorrow. And then after that, out to the compost pile.

Meanwhile, I can appreciate the pleasure I receive from looking at them. And I can bask in the thoughtfulness and love of my sweetie.

AGING TULIPS

By mid-April, winter is grasping at the covers, just as some dying people do. We had three nights of hard freezes, well down into the twenties. I thought the first night would be mild, but it wasn't. The next morning, the tulips on the front step were bowed over with the dowager humps of osteoporosis. They didn't straighten up again. The next two nights, I brought the ten pots of tulips indoors for hospice care. Since then, I've planted five pots in the ground. R.I.P., dear tulips.

Five more pots remain on the front step, looking a little unsteady on their feet but still blooming beautifully.

And so do we.

SMILING PANSIES

Pansies tremble in the chill April rain, but they like cool weather. Their adorable little faces look out at each April day, whether sunny or gray, no matter the adversity, and they say, *I'm happy to be alive. Aren't you?*

I have to agree. One morning, I listened to two cancer survivors talk with each other about how darn grateful they are for every single day. The grass is greener, right in their own backyard. Really! They feel more alive now than they did before their cancer diagnosis. Life is a miracle.

Isn't that odd? You stare death in the face and begin to really live your life. Contemplate your death today. While the pansies are smiling at you.

GARDENER'S NOSE

I went to the dermatologist to have her freeze a couple of spots on my face—a scaly spot and a red bump, both of which were precancerous. I asked her to look at my nose, which felt a bit rough. "Oh, you've got gardener's nose," she said.

Human skin, it turns out, is not beautiful. It's bumpy, scaly, rough in patches, and mine is a bit wrinkly. Look, really look at your skin with a magnifying glass. It's not actually pretty. No one's is.

At a recent meditation retreat, the monk/teacher led us through an abbreviated body meditation. He led us through a visualization of our skin. "Not beautiful." Then a visualization of our flesh. All I could imagine was the meat department at the grocery store. "Not beautiful," he said. Then our bones. "Not beautiful," he repeated.

Our skin is the saran wrap in which our body is covered. It peels, it scales off, it sweats, it wrinkles its nose. Our skin is the bag that holds the innards of our body together. Your bag looks like that; my bag looks like that, too.

I'm taking my bag of skin and my gardener's nose out to the garden to sniff the spring air and smell the flowers while I may.

COMPOST TO THE BRIM

The compost pile I'm adding to is full to the brim of the bin. Fortunately, every day it sinks an inch, like a freshly covered grave. Next day, I fill it to the top again. The compost pile I'm subtracting from is young. I can still see the remains of last summer's clean-up, when I ripped out a sizable patch of pachysandra and yanked out galloping ostrich ferns. The rhizomes of both are still completely recognizable. Only the green leaves have decomposed and disappeared.

I screen the young compost into a wheelbarrow and throw the chunky remains into the compost pile I'm adding to. Every day I fill it to the top. Every night, the heap sinks as if it's exhaling its last breath.

One of these days we too will be on the compost pile of life, with our cremains spread on land or water.

Until then, I enjoy the feel of the fresh, rich compost sifting through my fingers.

MANURE HAPPENS

My compost is young—less than a year old—and I'm going through it way too fast. I predict I could reach the bottom of my current pile in about a month, and then I'll be ready for the third pile, which I only finished last week. I am certain that a month-old pile will not be ready for me!

What to do? Install a temporary fourth compost bin. It was easier to convince my sweetie than I expected. He said "Yes" immediately. Into the new bin went a truckload of manure that I'd picked up the previous Saturday morning. I now have a compost pile completely made of manure. My hope is that, in a month, it will have decomposed into nice, rich dirt.

Sometimes it takes a while for us to compost the experience of our life. Images of the past come back to haunt us, just like the garbage in our compost pile. Then, years later, we wonder what all the fuss was about. Sigh. I spent weeks, months, years of my life on that? What a "waste" of time.

We all just need to age a little, digesting and composting our experience in order to make our lives richer and more fertile.

TICKS OFF

My forester neighbor, Lynn, took a friend out to the woods with her. Lynn was wearing permethrin-treated gaiters. When the two of them got back in the car, Lynn's friend had four ticks on her socks; Lynn had no ticks on her.

Okay. Now I'm serious about ticks. I have sprayed all my gardening clothes with permethrin, an anti-tick spray. It's probably the same stuff I used to spray all my clothes before I packed for India and again for Southeast Asia.

While some people bewail the multitude of ticks outdoors, I think of Lyme disease as our version of malaria. We have had the great good fortune to live in a safe area until just a few years ago. Now we join the rest of the world in having a nasty insect-borne disease right in our own backyard.

We are of the nature to become ill—whether or not we want to. My friends with Lyme disease have ongoing health issues. My heart goes out to them.

It's hard to have any sympathy at all for the ticks, but if they stay off me, they will have a much better chance of staying alive.

GOOD-BYE LAWN MOWER

It's time to trade in the lawn mower. It has become incontinent—leaking oil onto the garage floor. Even though it just had its annual physical exam at the hardware store a couple of months ago, it's now back there again, on life support. This faithful servant of 22 years has to be retired from service.

The man who is the mower of the lawn at my house still loves to ride around in green circles for an hour every other week. He's 78, and he probably doesn't have 22 years of service remaining. Nevertheless, he is choosing a new riding mower and continuing to serve his community in many different ways.

A SINGLE NIGHT

The night-blooming cereus blossoms for one night. Its petals begin springing open at dusk, and by dark the white flower is pumping out its perfume to attract nectar-feeding bats and certain moths. By dawn the flower is wilted, drooping forlornly. It's a short life for the night-blooming cereus flower. I keep the straggly succulent as a houseplant all year long just for this single night. (Thank goodness I was home!)

Our own bloom time is less than a single century. Yes, seventy, eighty, ninety, or one hundred years sounds like a long time when you are five or twenty or even thirty, but then various parts of the body start to wilt and droop—breasts, bellies, feet. The first wrinkle appears.

Oh, we are so beautiful. And then a new day dawns.

SEASONAL SHIFT

Nighttime temperatures drop into the thirties after fall equinox. It's time to think about making the seasonal change on the front step: bring the pots of annuals indoors and let magenta mums be the welcoming color for the next six weeks or so.

I watch as friends struggle with aging parents, trying to shift them into assisted living or perhaps a nursing home. Often the eighty-somethings don't want to make the change. Even if they are willing, the transition can feel difficult because so many things have to be let go of. One eighty-year-old friend broke into tears at the sight of the washing machine in her new condo near her daughter, a thousand miles away from "home." Her old washing machine, her usual washing machine, was gone. Gone.

We, too, might feel like shedding a tear. Summer is over. We enter the fall of our lives.

BRINGING THE FLOWERPOTS INDOORS

It's time to bring the flowerpots in from the front step and the back step. The first frost is coming in a few days. I have so enjoyed the luxuriant "welcome home" this summer of bright pink geraniums and variegated Swedish ivy.

Bringing the pots indoors is like putting them in a nursing home or a rehab center. Several of the plants get weaker and weaker over the winter, and finally give up the ghost. But most will survive in the solarium.

My gardening friend Ruth had a hip replacement five years ago and a knee replacement three years ago. She's working outdoors in her garden every hour that she can. She knows what the rehab center looks like—cooped up indoors for months.

Let's go out to our garden now. Today. And feel grateful for every minute we spend outdoors.

STOPPED FLOWERING

By mid-October, the geraniums in flowerpots outdoors have stopped flowering. I suspect their non-verbal message to me is, *Brrr. It's too cool out here. If I can't have more light, at least give me some more heat.*

I'm seeing a 95-year-old hospice client. Her hands are cold, so she has a heating pad muff to warm them up. She loves to fold clothes, hot out of the dryer. Her vision is so-so, and her mind is mostly gone. She's a sweet woman, and she keeps saying, "I want to go home."

Just like my geraniums.

REPRIEVE

Still no frost. Frost is predicted every night the third week of October, and still it doesn't freeze. Each day feels like a reprieve from a death sentence. A rally during the death vigil. How much longer? For death is coming to the garden. How could it not? Last evening, I made my last batch of basil pesto. The basil is gone. Well and truly gone.

But today, we have one more day, this day, to enjoy the tender annuals. One more day to pick pink zinnia and white dahlia bouquets. One more day to glean the last vegetables from the garden.

If you had one more day to live, how would you spend it? What would you do? How would you be? That one day is today. This moment. Now.

ALYSSUM STILL BLOOMS

In early November, alyssum is still blooming along the edges of several walkways. Despite the fact that it's November. Despite the fact that we have had hard frosts of 20 degrees. Despite the fact that it's dark out there. Alyssum is a real trouper.

In April, I buy three or five big packets of alyssum seed. Then I walk along the paths through the gardens and sprinkle. By June, the seeded ones have caught up with the ones that came from six-packs. And now, in November, when all the other annuals have given up the ghost, alyssum still blooms.

Alyssum soldiers on through the dark and difficult times, and emits a light, bouncy joy with its soft tiny white flowers. By this time of the year, it has spread into a little community.

A 75-year-old once said to me, "Aging feels like a battlefield. I look around at my fallen comrades. I don't understand why I'm still standing."

Alyssum still stands on the ground while the battle of aging, illness, and death goes on all around her.

PREPPING FOR WINTER

One of my three compost bins has been emptied out and all the compost spread on the vegetable garden. The triple benefit is:

- I now have one empty bin—a place to throw the winter's kitchen waste.
- The spring chore of spreading compost has already been done.
- Someone got some exercise and kept warm while she was shoveling out the compost bin.

November is a great time to do some spring chores, sort of like prepping for a big dinner party days (or months!) ahead.

How do we prep ourselves for our coming winter season?

- We can prune our collection of stuff. Recycle the stuff we haven't used in the past twelve months.
- We can focus on the mission statement of our lives. What's most important to the purpose of our life?
- Get some exercise.

Heavenly messengers are all around us, telling us about aging, illness, and death. One of their names is November. Another is Compost. Are we listening?

BLOOMING PINK

In mid-November, chard folds its colorful tents and disappears from the fall garden. That leaves kale and a lone snapdragon. I can't even grow snapdragons, yet there one is, hugging the ground and blooming, pink.

Cold weather crops (and flowers!) are few and far between. Single Johnny-jump-ups peek out here and there.

My 95-year-old hospice client complains of cold hands. "Oh, your hands are warm," she says when I greet her. She's always dressed in pink. After a while, she says, "I want to go home."

I've heard her daughters tell her many times she already *is* home, so I take a different tack. "Oh, when are you going home?" I ask.

"Soon," she says. "Soon."

PUTTING THE GARDEN TO BED

In mid-November, every person I meet asks, "Have you put your garden to bed?

I really don't want to say "yes." It's sort of feels like saying, "Yes, my dear friend the garden finally died this week." I want to eke out another day or two or maybe a week. But gardening chores are few and far between.

This week, when the snow tires are put on the car, is yet another indicator: Gardening season is over. Gone. Done.

Farewell, dear garden.

PASSÉ POPCORN

I finally took down the three little ears of popcorn that were decorating my front door. The chipmunks ate most of one ear, before I hung the three ears up out of the reach of their little paws.

In October, the gold and red popcorn looked so seasonal. In snowy December, it looks so passé. Our clothes that looked so sassy a few years ago now look out-of-style. Our bodies. . . Well, our bodies start to look a bit worse for wear, too.

Nevertheless, we keep decorating our bodies, trying to distract our attention, and the attention of other people, from the fact that we are becoming a bit passé ourselves. Our body has gone out of style. It has entered another season.

Still, we have deep gratitude for having a functioning body at all, regardless of how it looks. Even if it's eating popcorn.

DHARMA TALKS

IT'S ALL IN THE COMPANY YOU KEEP

As our morning meditation group dispersed, we were chatting about a young person we knew who had made a misstep, and Whit remarked, "It's all in the company you keep."

Oh yes! This aphorism reveals a deep Dharma teaching, sometimes referred to as "Noble Friends and Noble Conversations."

Our Dharma friends provide us with a rudder for navigating daily life, even though these "friends" may not keep our heart's closest company nor even meet much of our definition of "friend." At times, these people may feel more like "Dharma acquaintances" than "Dharma friends," yet it is our "noble conversations" with them that keep us on the straight and narrow with an actual decrease in the distress of our lives.

We can most easily see the effects of the company we keep in the teenagers we love. We hope and pray, bite our tongues, and wait anxiously as they navigate their peer groups in junior high and high school. We've seen and heard too many sad stories of teens seriously derailed by hanging out with the wrong crowd.

As we enter adulthood, perhaps we think that we ourselves are strong enough to be immune to such influences, but the company we keep still affects us deeply. Affinity with a group trumps intelligent, rational decision making.

One friend who married into a drinking family took up daily drinking because, she said, "I don't want to be ostracized." We don't want to lose our community, but we do need to choose wisely to begin with.

Take a close look at the company you keep. They may be fun, but are they admirable people?

Of course we love our friends, whether or not they are honorable. I once said to a Dharma teacher, "But I love my ignoble friends." Her advice: "Then be a noble friend to them." For the love we bear our friends, who may make their own unskillful choices, it's also all in the company they keep.

THE COMPLETE STREETS OF OUR SPIRITUAL PATH

In 1971, Oregon passed a law that all future streets and highways should be accessible to all sorts of wheeled vehicles like bicycles, wheelchairs, and strollers. Since then, sixteen states and 500 municipalities have passed this policy, which has come to be known as Complete Streets.

A complete street has bicycle lanes and sidewalks with curb cuts for accessibility. Other traffic-calming adjuncts like crosswalks, bulb-outs, and roundabouts increase safety for pedestrians. In some heavily trafficked communities, bicycle ridership on complete streets has increased by 500 percent and pedestrian/jogger use by 400 percent.

Our spiritual path can also be a "complete street" with three avenues for practice: daily life, weekly get-togethers with a sitting group, and, each year, at least one long retreat of at least three days.

The main thoroughfare of our practice is actually the time we spend with our spiritual friends. The Buddha tells us that our spiritual friends are "all of the spiritual life."

When we look at teenagers we love, we cross our fingers that they will fall in with the right peer groups. Peer groups are no less important for us as adults. Our friends and our nearest and dearest influence us tremendously. Actions are contagious, and we "catch" or copy the behaviors of those close to us.

Our spiritual friends can keep us from falling into the ditch on either side of the road we travel every day. Getting together with spiritual friends at least once a week, in a meditation or prayer group, for instance, is one of the keys to our spiritual progress.

Daily life for many of us is a crowded hubbub of places to go and people to see. Beginning our day with a few moments of solitude, meditation, or prayer can have a calming effect on the rest of our day.

An annual retreat is good for the maintenance of our mental vehicle. Taking time out for a long retreat inspires us to commit to meditate and gives us the confidence to continue on our way.

What's the complete street for your spiritual life? How much daily solitude? How much weekly sharing with spiritual friends? What traffic-calming devices can you set in place in your own daily life?

We don't want our busy lives to steamroller us, and we do want to set the wheel of Dharma rolling in our lives.

FORGIVE THEM

ONE OF MY SPIRITUAL teachers challenges me, once more, to forgiveness. You can't progress along the spiritual path if you're harboring resentments.

That makes sense to me, so, this Eastertide, I revisit my usual suspects—the old familiar grudges and dislikes. I know them very well. After all, I've lived with them for years.

I start collecting forgiveness phrases. *He could be right.* Even though I disagree with him about how he treats his mother—as if she's a duty that he discharges as infrequently as his conscience will allow. He visits her less and less often the older she gets.

He could be right.

Or I also like that familiar phrase of Jesus on the cross. *Forgive them for they know not what they do.* Forgive them because they are shortsighted. Forgive them because they are stupid. Forgive them because they are unconscious. Forgive them because they are greedy or aversive or delusional—just like all the rest of us.

Forgive them because they're teenagers or because they're old or because they're young.

Forgive them because they are thoughtless. Forgive them because they drink too much. Forgive them because they really don't have any idea what they are doing—either acts of commission or, more likely, acts of omission. Forgive them not because they're ungrateful, but because they simply take life for granted.

Forgive them.

IN CONCLUSION

Dear Connie,

Thank you for agreeing to take on the responsibility of holding my durable power of attorney for health care.

I want to put down on paper some of the images that guide me in my thinking about the bardo of dying, the cusp between life and death. My thinking about dying has been influenced by *The Tibetan Book of Living and Dying*, which I would recommend you read. If you have time to read only part of it, focus on chapters 11 through 15. Another book that has strongly affected me is *What Survives?* an anthology of essays about death.

For situations such as having a terminal condition, a persistent vegetative state, advanced loss of mental capability, incompetence, chronic illness, brain damage, and other such states, I request that I be given comfort care only. I do not want medical treatment, not even tube-feeding, to prolong my life. Or my so-called life.

I make these decisions about dying not from a depressed place, but from a place of great respect for life, or I should say, a place of great respect for life-death. Remember, I am a gardener who deals with the cycle of rebirth of perennials and bulbs, the birth of seeds, the growth of plants, and the death of plants and weeds. I throw uprooted plants and weeds into a compost pile. I don't think my physical form is any different.

A few months later that compost has become soil to nourish other plants.

In fact, one of my images has to do with the time between the first light frost and the killing frost which eventually does come. There are many cold-resistant plants—petunias, geraniums, alyssum—that limp along after the first frost. They basically stop blooming or have only one or two more flowers as the weather cools and never quite warms up again. I am not averse to pulling them out before the killing frost, even though they are still green. Likewise I am not averse to ending my life before the final killing frost of whatever illness or secondary illness. Uproot me from life supports. Pull the plug. Please do not continue to fertilize me with antibiotics, intravenous food, or liquids. Let Nature take its course.

I like the story of Scott Nearing, who, at 99, said one day to his wife Helen, "It's time to go." He stopped eating. After a while, he was still not "going," so he stopped taking all liquids. He died a few days before his 100th birthday.

I realize, of course, that I am writing this letter precisely because if I need a durable power of attorney for health care, I will not have reached 100, or 90 or 80 or 70. Even though I have not reached old, old age, I will say, "It's time to go." Let me go. I am willing to fast myself to death.

When I realized that my grandmother, Nonnie, had, essentially starved herself to death, I was appalled. It was hard for me, at age 39, to let her go. In retrospect, I have a great deal of respect for that approach. It's a kind of wild-animal way. I want to take that wild-animal way.

I think of Native Americans. When an elder could not travel on with the rest of the tribe, she was left behind with some water and some food, and was never seen again. If I am unable to travel on with my friends and family, please leave me behind.

I have learned that tube feeding and hydration increase pain and discomfort. First, there's getting the tubes in, and then there's excreting, which may mean more tubes for the outflow. Without tubes, after an initial period of discomfort that may last two or three days, the body begins to metabolize fat, ketones are produced, and the dying person feels no pain and may even feel euphoric. Sounds like a Vision Quest to me.

I would actually love to be taken out of the Intensive Care Unit and placed outdoors where I can hear the songs of birds and feel the touch of frost upon my cheeks and the breeze upon my face and body. Let me die of hypothermia. It's okay. At the least, bring me home. That will simplify my life-death and your decisions.

If I have some sort of dementia or brain damage, let me wander through the woods, a sort of walkabout. Don't go looking for me when I disappear. Either Providence will save me (like the time when Nathan was lost and he found Esther) or the wild animals will eat me. That's not a bad way to go—to lie down on a bed that Mother Earth has made.

My guiding motto is "Let Nature take its course." Please don't let medical care interfere with Nature.

Having a Christian Science father has affected my

outlook on this matter of life-death. A few hours after my father died, I found an open, empty bottle of sleeping pills on his bedside table. He did not want to prolong his or our (his children's) suffering.

Another aspect of this whole dying business that really irritates me is that the medical establishment is making money, lots of it, from me being sick. I am definitely *not* interested in my estate being eaten up by doctors and hospitals and lab tests and ambulances in the last few months of my life. I would much prefer that my money go to the people and organizations named in my will. My point of view is that, in general, doctors have a definite conflict of interest: they are earning money from the advice they give, urging us to accept their services.

Ideally, I would like to be comfortable and peaceful as "I" pass from this reality to another. Being given CPR, or being entubated, or getting shocked by paddles (as Hazel, your mother, was) does not qualify as a peaceful process. Please give a "Do Not Resuscitate" order and do NOT call Rescue.

What I value most about my life includes my relationships with friends. I value meditation.

My idea of death is that it is like being born into another reality. I don't know (and, oh, how I *love* knowing), but I am willing to go. Death is the goal of life.

> "When you were born, you died, and the world rejoiced.
> Live your life so, that when you die, the world cries and you rejoice."

I obviously do not believe that life should be prolonged as long as possible. Quality of life is very important to me. If I am unaware of my life and surroundings, if I am unable to appreciate and continue the important relationships in my life, unable to think well enough to make everyday decisions, or if I am in severe pain or discomfort, please do not use life-prolonging treatment, not even antibiotics.

The only reason for temporarily accepting medical treatment is so that my family and friends feel better, so that they have minimal regrets. As far as I am concerned, it is okay to leave some stones unturned. Healing can mean dying.

If my chances for recovering from an illness or injury are good (50–50 or better), I do have some tolerance for pain. I think of myself as a risk-taker, so my advice is to take the risk.

If my chances are poor (less than 10 percent), please give me comfort care only.

I shudder at the knowledge that it takes months for the doctor to declare a persistent vegetative state. I could be in a plain old vegetative state for months before they call it persistent. My reaction to difficult end-of-life situations, such as are in the news, is this: If friends and family want to withdraw life supports, they should be able to. They have already agonized over the decision, and they know best.

I would like for you to consider holistic alternatives. A daily massage might feel good. Ask friends to come, and, assuming I can hear, give me meditation instruction.

Claire Stanley has clarity, so I would really like for her to come.

I realize there is an entire realm of situations that I have not thought of. I leave you with the vast gray area between poor chances (less than 10 percent) and good chances (50–50 or better). I trust your ability, your advocacy, and your research. And most of all I trust your intuition.

I will never forget the time I was very upset about my written evaluation at the Council on Aging (1978). I called you in tears. You told me some story about being on a plane in Malaysia. The announcement was made that the windshield wipers didn't work, and there would be a slight delay. When you asked if they were getting a new part, the reply was, "No, we're getting a new pilot." Minutes later, as I sat through my face-to-face evaluation, on the verge of more tears, I looked down at my pad of paper and my pen whose label read "Pilot." I had to smile.

Ever since that experience (and many other similar ones), I deeply trust your intuition. In choosing you as my durable power of attorney for health care, I trust that you will pilot me through a time when I am unable to make my own decisions.

With love,
Cheryl

www.ingramcontent.com/pod-product-compliance
Lightning Source LLC
Chambersburg PA
CBHW030443300426
44112CB00009B/1133